ONE HU...
SEX
SCENES
THAT CHANGED CINEMA

NEIL FULWOOD

B T BATSFORD

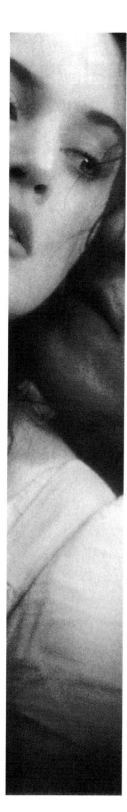

For Paul Rowe

AUTHOR'S NOTE

This book focuses on scenes from 100 films that have had an effect on sexual representation in cinema. In order to provide context, it has been necessary to mention a number of other films. Therefore, the 100 films under specific discussion are identified in the text in boldface.

All stills courtesy of The Joel Finler Picture Collection, except for those on pages 11 and 13, which are from the author's own collection.

First published 2003
© Neil Fulwood 2003
The right of Neil Fulwood to be identified as the author of this work has been asserted by him in accordance with the Copyright, Designs and Patents Act 1988.

ISBN 0 7134 8858 1

A CIP catalogue record for this book is available from the British Library.

Printed in Spain
for the publishers
B T Batsford Ltd
The Chrysalis Building
Bramley Road
London W10 6SP
www.batsford.com

An imprint of **Chrysalis** Books Group plc

Distributed in the United States and Canada by Sterling Publishing Co., 387 Park Avenue South, New York, NY 10016, USA

CONTENTS

CHAPTER THREE: THE EUROPEAN AESTHETIC   83

CHAPTER FOUR: PLEASURE AND PAYMENT   107

CHAPTER FIVE: FORBIDDEN FLESH   137

AFTERWORD   153

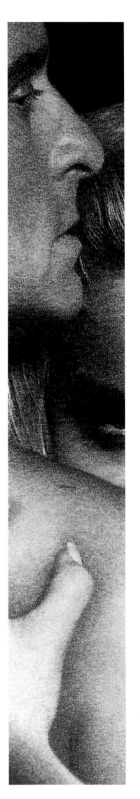

implicit

CHAPTER ONE

Picture the setting, not that it's particularly romantic or erotic: a run-down diner/gas station somewhere in the sticks, a sign out front reading 'MAN WANTED'. The proprietor is a shambolic middle-aged drunkard; the business is starved of customers.

Into this milieu comes Frank Chambers (John Garfield), a drifter and self-confessed 'cheap nobody'; so begins **The Postman Always Rings Twice** (Tay Garnett, 1946). He enters into dialogue with the proprietor, Nick Smith (Cecil Kellaway), who offers him a job and a hamburger on the house. They go inside to discuss terms and conditions. Nick leaves Frank to tend to the stove while he goes to serve someone waiting for petrol on the forecourt.

Across the floor, bare of carpeting, rolls a tube of lipstick. It comes to rest at Frank's feet. The camera tracks back, reaching an open door, which frames a tanned and shapely pair of legs. A quick pan up and we are presented with an archetypal film noir scenario: the introduction of the *femme fatale*; the promise of the erotic; the moment where the hero's fate is sealed.

Archetypal film noir: John Garfield ensnared by Lana Turner in *The Postman Always Rings Twice*.

Not that Frank is much of a hero. Nor is film noir a genre in which heroes are prevalent. Indeed, the usual motivations of film noir characters are greed, lust or fear. The men, for all their tendencies towards violence, are often weak; they allow themselves to be manipulated by women. That the *femmes fatales* are the stronger characters owes in no small part to their use of sexual self-awareness as their weapon of choice.

The *femme fatale* here is Cora Smith (Lana Turner), wife of the hapless Nick, and sole beneficiary under the terms of his will. As the film progresses, she will inveigle Frank's help in murdering him, the quicker to acquire his business and profit from his life insurance policy. And from the outset, it is evident that Frank is going to do her bidding. His first interaction with Cora – completely non-verbal – tells us all we need to know. She stands framed in the doorway, watching him coolly. Her outfit – a revealing top and shorts, almost as if she were dressed for the beach – is as white as her motives are dark. Frank picks up the tube of lipstick and hands it to her. She glosses her lips right in front of him, still eyeing him insouciantly, then turns away. The hamburger burns on the stove as he gawps after her.

Not only is the scene loaded with unspoken tension between the characters; it also acts as a metaphor for the film entire. The tube of lipstick equates to the favours Cora will bestow on Frank should he do her bidding; the area of floor it rolls across represents the property Cora schemes to get her hands on; and the conflagration on the stove symbolizes (albeit unsubtly) the heat of their passion and the violent act that will ultimately destroy them.

The promise of the erotic: suggestion and manipulation in film noir

Billy Wilder's **Double Indemnity** (1944) is very much the precursor of *The Postman Always Rings Twice* – unsurprisingly, since both were based on novels by James M Cain[1]. Again a culpable male, insurance salesman Walter Neff (Fred MacMurray), is beguiled by a predatory female, Phyllis Dietrichson (Barbara Stanwyck), intent on reaping the rewards of her husband's premature demise. In a plot twist more coldly cynical than anything *Postman* has to offer, Neff is made complicit even before the murder when Phyllis persuades him to take out the policy (the film's title derives from the accidental death clause) without her husband's knowledge.

Like Cora, she uses Neff's attraction to her in order to manipulate him. But whereas Cora's ploys are entirely physical (she is constantly applying lip gloss, smoking cigarettes in a manner that draws attention to her lips or flouncing around in beach wear), with Phyllis, notwithstanding that she is introduced wearing just a towel, there is a more intellectual edge. Whereas Cora leads her accomplice on, Phyllis sounds him out. Neff meets Phyllis when he arrives at her house to discuss car insurance with her husband. The husband is conveniently out. Phyllis appears at the top of the stairs, betowelled. During the course of the scene, they twice base their conversation around metaphors. The first plays on Neff's line of work.

Neff: I'd hate to think of you getting a scratched fender when you're not covered.
Phyllis: I know what you mean. I've been sunbathing.
Neff: Hope there weren't any pigeons around.

The erotic connotations of 'not covered' (unclothed) are reinforced by Phyllis choosing this moment to withdraw to her room to change. She reappears, still buttoning up her dress, and slowly descends the stairs. The camera lingers on her ankle-bracelet (traditionally a piece of jewellery associated with prostitution). The implication of voyeurism in Neff's comment about pigeons is here made manifest.

Their second bout of metaphor-laden verbal sparring comes when Neff makes it clear that he has less interest in returning later to speak with her husband, and more in actually seeing her again. Phyllis castigates him for going too fast (i.e. being too insistent).

Phyllis: There's a speed limit in this state. 45 miles an hour.
Neff: How fast was I going, officer?
Phyllis: I'd say about 90.
Neff: Suppose you get down off that motorcycle and give me a ticket.
Phyllis: Suppose I give you a warning instead.
Neff: Suppose it doesn't take.
Phyllis: Suppose I have to rap you over the knuckles.
Neff: Suppose I burst out crying and put my head on your shoulder.
Phyllis: Suppose you put it on my husband's shoulder.

Suggestive stuff. The main implication is that Neff already sees himself as subservient to her. Also, the choice of a legal infraction (albeit a minor one) as metaphor tells us they will soon be partners in crime. But most of all, there is the sense of Phyllis working out an angle – how she can use Neff to her best advantage – even as she weaves her seductive web.

Charles Vidor's **_Gilda_** (1946) serves up just as much erotic tension. Indeed, Rita Hayworth's performance as the eponymous object of desire is so central to the film's aesthetic – so defining – that the narrative (a tangled tale of loyalty, betrayal, casinos and cartels) is shunted so far into the background as to be superfluous.

If *The Postman Always Rings Twice* and *Double Indemnity* can be said to revolve around the eternal triangle – husband, wife, lover – Gilda ups the ante by setting its protagonists in a *ménage a trois* of sorts. The story begins with small-time gambler Johnny Farrell (Glen Ford) rescued by casino boss Ballin Mundson (George Macready) from a sure-fire beating after cheating at dice. Mundson, elegant but contemptuous, hires Farrell to keep his casino free of fellow cheats. A close relationship develops. The sense of latent homoeroticism is summarized by Mundson's comment, 'women and gambling don't mix'.

It isn't long, though, before Gilda comes between them.

The *femme fatale* as icon: Rita Hayworth in *Gilda*.

When Mundson returns from a business trip, newly married to her following a whirlwind romance, he does not realize that she and Farrell have a history. Gilda mocks Farrell from the outset, calling him a 'boy'. Mundson, unaware of the reason behind her hostility, soon begins treating him in the same manner.

Tension is heightened when Mundson, treating his wife as no better than a kept woman, alters Farrell's job description: henceforth, he becomes her personal chauffeur/minder. 'Picking up the boss's laundry,' as Gilda puts it, a line steeped in self-loathing even though it is an accusation against Farrell.

Plot twists pile up: there is an assassination attempt on Mundson; he later fakes his own death. Against all this, the sexual power games between the three leads remain at the forefront, and it is Gilda who provides the most erotic moment – a scene in which two long black gloves are the only items of clothing removed – when she upstages both men at Mundson's casino, performing a burlesque rendition of 'Put the Blame on Mame'.

'There never was a woman like Gilda' screams the tagline on the poster – and this scene pretty much licences the hyperbole. Clad in a sleek black number that is low-cut to the point of defying gravity, peeling off the aforementioned gloves and tossing them into the crowd (choreographer Jack Cole allegedly modelled the dance numbers on those of a striptease artiste of his acquaintance), Hayworth performs the routine with a sense of wild abandon[2]. As the song ends, Gilda unclips her diamond necklace and throws that to the cheering horde of admirers, then makes the provocative comment, 'I'm not very good with zippers.'

That the scene generates such *frisson* owes to the centrality of its smouldering *femme fatale*: it is at this point that everything in the film – its characters, its plot contrivances – are held in stasis, subjugated to Gilda's display of sensual self-expression. It also demonstrates the use of music and dance in on-screen sexuality.

Torch numbers: sexual expression in music and dance

The music to which Gilda performs her routine is a big band number, allowing for smoky, torch-style vocals as well as large slabs of brass and percussion conducive to bump-and-grind dance moves. Forty years on, a torch song – this time with just a piano accompaniment – provides **The Fabulous Baker Boys** (Steve Kloves, 1989) with its most iconic moment. Again, the dynamic is the arrival of a woman, which upsets a close relationship between two men.

The men here are brothers: Jack and Frank Baker (Jeff and Beau Bridges respectively). They are professional pianists, though nowhere near the Alfred Brendel league. Gigging at upmarket bars and lounges, their programme of light jazz and nostalgic conversation between numbers is less than inspiring. To keep from losing bookings, they reluctantly take on a singer. Enter Susie Diamond (Michelle Pfeiffer), a former escort girl with a laconic attitude that mirrors Jack's approach to life. Her presence exacerbates an already volatile sense of resentment between Frank, a dedicated family man and the business brains of the outfit, and Jack, who cares about nothing except his dog, and takes his only pleasure playing for nothing in low-lit jazz clubs the wrong side of midnight.

The film reaches its turning point at a rural hotel where the threesome is playing a New Year's gig. The brothers' non-communication, played out in counterpoint to the increasing sexual tension between Jack and Susie, is made manifest when Frank is called away by an emergency on New Year's Eve. Jack and Susie are left to perform the set themselves. They lose no time in dropping Frank's preferred musical programme – hoary old standards like 'Feelings' – and go for something sexier. What better song than 'Makin' Whoopee'? Forget the raised-eyebrow sense of *double entendre* with which most male vocalists imbue it (one thinks of Frank Sinatra's version on the *Songs for Swingin' Lovers* album); Susie delivers it in low, sultry, come-hither tones. The sexual references abounding in the lyrics are emphasized by the sight of a semi-recumbent Susie, all red dress and high heels, draped across Jack's grand piano.

Michelle Pfeiffer as lounge singer Susie Diamond in *The Fabulous Baker Boys.*

As with *Gilda*, the narrative halts in order to give the female protagonist (quite literally) centre stage. But whereas the musical interlude in Vidor's film is solely about Gilda, what we are seeing here demonstrates the chemistry between Jack and Susie: at one point, she caresses his face while he plays; at the close of the song, she climbs down from the piano and leans against him, head thrown back, as he picks out the last few notes. The dynamic of this scene is based entirely on the tension and contact between pianist and singer – man and woman – and signposts the subsequent narrative development whereby one seduces the other. It is the fractious nature of this sexual relationship that leads to the disintegration of their act and the final rift between Jack and Frank, the dramatic *mise en scènes* that inform the latter half of the film.

A quite different turning point is reached when **From Dusk Till Dawn** (Robert Rodriguez, 1996) delivers its big musical number. There is a different flavour to the music – Tex-Mex and slightly seedy – and the scene serves as a prelude to something that is decidedly un-erotic. Rodriguez's film, from a script by Quentin Tarantino (who co-stars), is very much a game of two halves. It starts out as a conventional crime thriller: two brothers, Seth (George

13

Clooney) and Richie (Tarantino) flee to Mexico with a suitcase full of ill-gotten money, a trail of murdered policemen and innocent bystanders left in their wake. To facilitate an easier border crossing, they kidnap a family and hide in their recreational vehicle. Once out of the United States, they make their captives drive them to an out-of-the-way roadhouse, the Titty Twister, where they have arranged to meet their contact.

As its name suggests, the Titty Twister is a sleazy establishment, frequented by rough customers. Its main attractions are a live band and a group of topless dancers. When Seth and Richie arrive, their hostages in tow, they are just in time for the highlight of the evening's entertainment, an appearance by the cryptically named Santanico Pandemonium (Salma Hayek). At the conclusion of her performance, the film changes direction in mid-stream (the scene comes at almost exactly the halfway mark) and bloodily embraces all the traditions and iconography of the vampire genre. The dance number bridges these differing aesthetics. As with *Gilda*, it is a moment of narrative stasis; and like *The Fabulous Baker Boys*, it generates its own internal dynamic.

Santanico appears on a stage that looks more like a pagan altar, flames shimmering to either side of her. The set design is redolent of old Hammer studios productions, a pointer to the ensuing shift in genre. She wears little more than a bikini and a cape. She removes the cape almost immediately, to reveal a snake wrapped around her. Not only does the snake provide another point of reference for horror movie enthusiasts, but also its phallic symbolism speaks for itself. The music begins, guitar-driven, the vocal barely a murmur, and Santanico dances. The snake is removed and she makes her way off the stage, onto the tables around which the Titty Twister's lascivious clientele are grouped.

Gilda's routine is evocative of striptease; Santanico's quite literally becomes a table dance. The finale has her interacting with the audience, reaching down to pick up Richie's bottle of beer, which she then pours down the smooth expanse of one leg. Richie licks the beer off her foot appreciatively. The music ends; applause rings out. 'Now that,' Seth comments, 'is what I call a fucking show.'

It is at this point that *From Dusk Till Dawn* effects its transition: reacting to the blood seeping from a wound Richie has earlier sustained, Santanico is revealed as a vampire and – pardon the pun – pandemonium ensues.

At the risk of drawing a crass analogy, it can be said that Santanico's sexuality unleashes a destructiveness that affects those around her (as do Gilda and Susie Diamond, only without going to the extreme of turning into vampires). Metaphorically, this is borne out by the presence of the snake, imbued as it is with connotations of the serpent in the Garden of Eden. It signals an end to Seth and Richie's paradise (everything has gone their way so far: they've got away with the money, evaded the authorities and successfully crossed the border) and the beginning of their own personal hell (Seth is forced to kill his brother when he becomes one of the undead, the first victim of Santanico's attack).

From Dusk Till Dawn is as different a movie to *The Fabulous Baker Boys* as it is to *Gilda*, but all three draw upon a synthesis of dance, music and sexual expression that stretches back (ironically, since music is an aural medium) to silent film. **Pandora's Box** (G W Pabst, 1928), aptly described by Maitland McDonagh as 'a morality tale with no moral'[3], uses a dance sequence to make its strongest statement about its heroine's need to demonstrate her sexual self-identity. So strong is this need, that Lulu (Louise Brooks) ultimately causes the downfall of everyone around her – as well as sealing her own fate.

The first half of the film highlights her less-than-auspicious background – her association with Schigolch (Carl Gotz), the pimp who exploited her in her youth, and whose company she still keeps (perversely, she passes him off at one point as her father) – as well as her talent for beguiling admirers into keeping her in the manner to which she is accustomed. Her meal ticket when the film opens is newspaper owner Peter Schon (Fritz Kortner), whose son Alwa (Franz Lederer) is himself carrying a torch for her. She disrupts his engagement to a socially more suitable woman, publicly seducing him. Compromised, left with no choice but to marry Lulu, Schon discovers that while he might have financed her lifestyle he certainly doesn't own her. She chooses their wedding celebrations to make this point.

Dressed in inappropriately virginal white, she gives her new husband short shrift, instead flattering Schigolch with her attentions, behaving enticingly towards Alwa, and dancing an intimate tango with the openly lesbian aristocrat Countess Anna Geschwitz (Alice Roberts). The Countess's silken black dress is in stark contrast to the white of Lulu's; likewise her butch appearance – only the feminine outfit saves her from androgyny – is at odds with Lulu's shimmering persona. Always feminine, always seductive, she vacillates between the coquette and the vamp, sometimes within the space of moments.

The scene is tense enough given the degree of humiliation Schon suffers (cold-shouldered while his bride comes on to first a pimp, and then his own son); but what really electrifies it is the sudden suggestion that Lulu's promiscuity extends to other women, making her arguably the first heroine in cinema to consciously define her own sexuality rather than being defined or objectified by the male characters who surround her. It also presents one of cinema's earliest instances of sapphic sexual chemistry, prefiguring same-sex dancefloor scenes in *The Conformist* (Bernardo Bertolucci, 1969) and *Bitter Moon* (Roman Polanski, 1992).

Stand-ins: metaphor in dialogue and imagery

As we have seen in *Double Indemnity*, dialogue based around a metaphor can communicate sexual tension between characters without recourse to the explicit. Through reasons of censorship or, as we shall see in the more contemporary examples cited later in this chapter, the acquisition of a less strident rating (generally conducive to better box office), many films use similar ploys.

In ***Spartacus*** (Stanley Kubrick, 1960), bisexuality is rendered in culinary terms. The scene is set in such a way that there can be no evasion of the homoeroticism on display. General Crassus (Laurence Olivier) calls for his servant Antoninus (Tony Curtis) to bathe him. He sits upright in a sunken bath, his entire torso above the waterline. Antoninus, stripped to the waist, is compelled to step into the bath; physical contact is necessitated. (The camera dwells on Curtis's muscular physique throughout.) A curtain of fine material is drawn around Crassus's bathing room, lending the proceedings a voyeuristic quality. The general asks Antoninus if he has ever stolen, lied or 'dishonoured the gods'. Antoninus replies that he has not. Crassus steers the conversation in another direction:

> **Crassus:** Do you refrain from these vices out of respect for moral virtues?
> **Antoninus:** Yes, master.
> **Crassus:** Do you eat oysters?
> **Antoninus:** When I have them, master.
> **Crassus:** Do you eat snails?
> **Antoninus:** No, master.

Crassus: Do you consider the eating of oysters to be moral and the eating of snails to be immoral?
Antoninus: No, master.
Crassus: Of course not. It is all a matter of taste … and taste is not the same as appetite and therefore not a question of morals, is it?
Antoninus: It could be argued so, master.
Crassus: My taste includes both snails and oysters.

The repeated use of 'master' in Antoninus's responses imbues him with a submissiveness that his physical strength belies. The way Crassus phrases his questions – the concept of 'taste' being 'not a question of morals' is a snippet of double-speak worthy of a lawyer – suggests that he is setting out to coerce Antoninus. The portrait of Crassus as a libertine, eager for any form of sexual delectation or experimentation, is completed when he declares his affinity for 'both snails and oysters'.

This is a prime example of how an emotionally complex and sexually charged scene is rendered in terms conducive to censorial lenience. There is nothing explicit here: the physical contact occurs in an historically accurate context (those of high rank or social standing were bathed by servants); the dialogue is literate and eloquent, never profane. Yet there remains no doubt as to Crassus's prurience, or his designs on Antoninus.

The irony, of course, is for all that Kubrick and scriptwriter Dalton Trumbo avoided the explicit, the scene was cut from the original theatrical release. It was not until the film was restored in 1991 that it was reinstated. The footage was retrieved, but the soundtrack was missing. Tony Curtis, then aged 66, re-recorded his dialogue. Olivier, however, had died two years earlier; Anthony Hopkins stepped in, seamlessly emulating Olivier's vocal qualities.

No less provocative a subject for its time was the atmosphere of barely repressed sexual hysteria depicted in Powell and Pressburger's **Black Narcissus** (1947). The first of their collaborations not to be rooted in wartime propaganda – and their first production since the 'love conquers all' romantic fantasy of *A Matter of Life and Death* (1946) – this adaptation of Rumer Godden's novel couldn't have been any more different from their filmography to date. There is no wartime backdrop; no 'message'; no romanticism.

The story opens with Sister Clodagh (Deborah Kerr), a devout nun serving at a mission in the Himalayas, charged with establishing

an order in a decaying old building precipitously founded on the edge of a sheer mountainside. From here on in, every frame of film is suffused with a dark sexuality: the property is revealed as a former brothel, suggestive frescos still adorning the walls; the gardens overflow with exotic flora (a more subtle Garden of Eden metaphor than that in *From Dusk Till Dawn*); the schoolroom is filled to bursting with local children (evidence that procreation is rife in the surrounding villages). The agent for the property, Mr Dean (David Farrar), evinces a darkly sexual persona: he is ruggedly handsome, and steeped in machismo – as well as being a hard drinker, he is direct to the point of abrupt; he is certainly no gentleman. His presence, more than any other factor, contributes to the growing tension between the nuns.

Elsewhere, the almost-developed sexuality of orphaned Indian girl Kanchi (Jean Simmons, cast against type but utterly compelling) is contrasted with the ludicrous adolescent pretence at sophistication attempted by Dilip Rai (Sabu), the son of the Himalayan general who has permitted the nuns residency in the former bordello. (The film takes its title from the imported cologne the boy wears.) Nonetheless, this unlikely couple lose no time in eloping.

Tensions run high between the nuns. The volatile Sister Ruth (Kathleen Byron), torn between her duty and her desires, refuses to renew her vows and determines to leave the mission. In the film's most startling scene, Clodagh visits Ruth in her cell. Ruth has divested herself of her habit and is wearing a red dress. Biblically, there is an association of scarlet with wantonness. This is compounded when Clodagh, insisting on staying with Ruth till morning (when she is due to leave), reads piously from the Bible. Clodagh is convinced that she can persuade Ruth against her decision. Ruth responds by taunting Clodagh, distracting her from the pages of the Good Book as she applies a coating of lipstick as red as her dress. Ruth's already undisguised attraction to Dean is one thing (his subsequent rejection of her paves the way for her attack on Clodagh in the film's vertiginous finale), but her overtures to Clodagh take *Black Narcissus* into a quite different realm. If her red dress (cf. *The Fabulous Baker Boys*) denotes her free-spiritedness, and the lipstick (cf. *The Postman Always Rings Twice*) serves to accentuate her looks, the fact that she uses these visual prompts on another woman – and does so with a certain degree of success (Clodagh experiences flashbacks to her only romantic relationship) – suffuses the scene with similar implications to Crassus and Antoninus's dialogue in *Spartacus*.

Visual metaphors in *Black Narcissus*, then, carry a psychological import. But they can also be used for humorous purposes. Billy Wilder's **Some Like it Hot** (1959), a razor-sharp satire involving gangsters and transvestitism, is arguably one of the most elegant comedies of sexual mores ever to have emerged from Hollywood. Reluctant witnesses to the St Valentine's Day massacre, jazz musicians Joe (Tony Curtis) and Jerry (Jack Lemmon) go on the run from mob boss Spats Columbo (George Raft). An opening for a sax and a bass player in an orchestra booked to appear at a swish Florida hotel gives them the ticket out of Chicago they need. One problem: it's an all-girl outfit. Solution: dress in drag, speak falsetto and adopt the names Josephine and Daphne.

Complications, of course, ensue: Joe falls for dipsomaniac lead singer Sugar Kane (Marilyn Monroe), ageing playboy Osgood Fielding (Joe E Brown) falls for Jerry, and the Friends of Italian Opera (read: the Mob) show up in Florida for a convention of crooks. The Joe/Sugar, Jerry/Osgood flirtation – played out in parallel – provides the main comic set-pieces. Joe divests himself of the accoutrements of Josephine at the earliest opportunity and adopts another disguise, this time as a Cary Grant-style smoothie. He attracts Sugar by appealing to her sense of materialism, passing himself off as heir to the Shell Oil fortune. With Jerry forced to maintain his Daphne persona in order to lure Osgood from his yacht, Joe takes Sugar aboard the vessel. In a nifty reversal of the typical seduction scene, he claims an inability to make love to women. Consequently, Sugar takes matters in hand. Draping herself across him (he is reclining on a couch), she kisses him passionately.

Sugar: Anything?

Joe: I'm afraid not. Terribly sorry …

Sugar: You're not giving yourself a chance … Relax. [She kisses him again.]

Joe: Like smoking without inhaling.

Sugar: Don't inhale.

As witty as the interplay is between the leads (and Monroe's comic timing is impeccable), what makes the scene hilarious is Joe's leg rising behind Sugar the first time she kisses him. Not only does this serve the narrative purpose of revealing his true feelings (the film, after all, is built around masquerade and false identity), but also it's a sly and debonair manner of suggesting an erection.

In Joseph Losey's ***The Servant*** (1963), the suggestion is made of a homosexual relationship, notwithstanding that the main characters are ostensibly heterosexual. This subtext is smuggled in beneath the film's primary narrative purpose: an investigation of class and power.

Master and servant: distortion and role reversal in *The Servant.*

The flunkey of the title, Hugo Barrett (Dirk Bogarde) is taken on by Tony (James Fox[4]), a young man whose aristocratic good looks belie the fact that he is nouveau riche, lazy and weak-willed. Barrett quickly begins to usurp his authority, a ploy suspected by Tony's fiancée Susan (Wendy Craig). Barrett cajoles Tony into hiring Vera (Sarah Miles), a woman he announces as his sister, as a maid. An indiscretion while Barrett is ostensibly attending his sick mother leads to a one-night stand between Tony and Vera.

Concerned that Tony is being manipulated, Susan moves in with him and starts treating Barrett high-handedly. Matters come to a head when Tony and Susan return earlier than expected from a weekend away and discover Barrett and Vera having sexual relations. Barrett reveals that she is not his sister, but his fiancée, remarking that this turn of events 'sort of puts us in the same boat, sir'. This revelation effectively terminates Tony and Susan's engagement, and Tony dismisses Barrett.

Drinking heavily following Susan's departure, Tony later rehires Barrett (Barrett claims that Vera has left him, and that she used them both). This is the turning point. Roles become reversed. Barrett's obsequious 'sir' (equivalent to Antoninus's 'yes master') is replaced by 'mate' and 'Tone'. They bicker like an old married couple. An oblique remark to shared experiences in the army hints at homosexual activities in their past.

At the denouement, Barrett throws a party. The guests comprise a few shabby-looking women who may or may not be prostitutes. Drunkenness and indifferent use of these women are the order of the day. Vera shows up, seemingly to beg money from Tony; however, she soon enters into the spirit of things. It is through her presence that the subtext of repressed homosexuality is consolidated. She is the woman both men have used (despite Barrett's allegations that *she* is the predator). Through her they have had sex by proxy. Just as they intend to do with the less than salubrious female company Barrett has procured for the party.

Things are curtailed, though, by the arrival of Susan. Evidently still concerned about her ex, she is shocked at his state of inebriation, and how freely he is giving himself over to the favours on offer. In a last-ditch attempt to recapture his attention/affections, she makes a move on Barrett. He rejects her. The slap she gives him as she leaves – and the shaky, effeminate way he reacts – identifies Barrett as a stand-in for 'the other woman', the third party who has driven a wedge into her relationship with Tony. The film ends with Barrett herding everyone out; the final image is of him and Tony alone, no women between them any longer.

Less sophisticated, but nonetheless effective, examples of metaphor are scattered throughout mainstream cinema. Take **From Here to Eternity** (1953), Fred Zinneman's adaptation of James Jones's novel about American soldiers (and their various romantic entanglements) stationed in Honolulu on the eve of the Japanese attack on Pearl Harbor. Although a very sanitized version (the novel is frank in its depiction of sex, brutality and racism), the film still gets across Jones's criticism of the military system.

A synopsis presents a cross-section of corrupt hierarchy: a young enlisted man, Robert Prewitt (Montgomery Clift), refuses to box for the regiment, earning himself the disapprobation of Captain Holmes (Philip Ober), who instructs Sergeant Warden (Burt Lancaster) to make his life hell. Warden (an apt name given the prison-like disciplinary excesses that characterize life at the barracks) happily complies, while at the same time cuckolding Holmes by carrying on an affair with his wife, Karen (Deborah Kerr).

The Warden/Karen relationship mirrors that of Prewitt and the girl he falls for, Lorene (Donna Reed), a nightclub hostess (a polite Hollywood euphemism of the time for hooker) whose fantasies of being an officer's wife tip over into self-delusion. But whereas Prewitt and Lorene's tentative relationship is hardly the stuff of grand cinematic melodrama, the scenes between Warden and Karen practically beg the definition 'tempestuous'. Their most memorable encounter provides the film's key image. To a backdrop of thunderous waves, they scramble down a rocky escarpment to a secluded area of beach. Warden strips down to his shorts. Karen pulls off her skirt; she is wearing a one-piece bathing suit. They race into the sea. Zinneman renders this imagery all the more feral for intercutting it with Prewitt brooding jealously over Lorene's attentions to other men at the club. When he cuts back to Warden and Karen, they are lying in close embrace, lips together, as the surf crashes around them.

Using a metaphor that is just as unsubtle, **Tom Jones** (Tony Richardson, 1963) also invokes *Spartacus* in its food-fixation, but in this case dialogue is abandoned in favour of the purely visual. Based on Henry Fielding's rambunctious novel, Albert Finney stars as the inveterate ladies' man of the title. The film starts with its hero abandoned as a baby at the estate of Squire Allworthy (George Devine). Allworthy assumes the child to be the offspring of two of his servants, Jenny Jones (Joyce Redman) and Partridge (Jack MacGowran). Outraged as much by their unmarried status as by the actual abandonment of the child, he dismisses them and undertakes to bring Tom up as if he were his own son. Allworthy, however, does have a son of his own, Blifil (David Warner). Blifil's sense of Tom as a rival continues into adolescence as Tom proves popular with women and indulges to the fullest in the many sexual favours he is offered.

Despite all these dalliances, Tom's affections are reserved for the high-born Sophie Western (Susannah York). Sophie's aunt, the priggish Miss Western (Edith Evans), is aware of Tom's dubious parentage and makes no bones about her disapproval. She tries to coerce Sophie into a marriage with Blifil, a ploy that is foiled when she publicly declares her love for Tom. Her father, Squire Western

(Hugh Griffith), responds to the ensuing social embarrassment by having Tom framed for a crime of which he is blameless. Allworthy, also concerned that his social standing will be affected, exiles Tom to London. Here, his womanizing ways get him into yet more trouble and the film edges towards its denouement with Tom in the shadow of the noose[5].

It is during his journey to the capital that Tom meets Jenny Jones, older but no less buxom, now calling herself Mrs Waters. She doesn't know who he is; he doesn't know that she is rumoured to be his mother (she isn't – Allworthy's sister is revealed, at the end of the film, as having given birth to him). The instant attraction between them, uncomfortable as it is to watch when one is not aware of this twist, is demonstrated in the infamous meal scene. Across a table practically groaning with food, they stare into each others' eyes – not in a dreamy, sentimental way, but communicating an utterly basic need – as they consume their meal in an equally carnal manner. The phrase 'consuming passion' springs readily to mind. Moreover, it doesn't take a great leap of the imagination to link the juices that run from their lips with the implication of oral sex.

For all of its bawdiness, *Tom Jones* is not an explicit film. Ironically, one of cinema's most ungainly metaphors features in a PG-rated melodrama whose approach to its characters' sexuality is almost chaste. **Ghost** (Jerry Zucker, 1990) is every inch an old-fashioned weepie. Its leads, Sam (Patrick Swayze) and Molly (Demi Moore) are young, attractive and very much in love. He's a financial executive; she's the sensitive artistic type (she sculpts). They've just moved into a magnificent apartment. But, as with every example of this lachrymose genre, there is an impediment to their happiness; indeed, to them being together.

In short, Sam dies, in an 'accident', leaving Molly to the predatory advances of Sam's supposed best friend Carl (Tony Goldwyn). Who, it turns out, was complicit in Sam's demise. Of course, it never gets too unpleasant: Sam protects Molly from beyond the grave, ensuring that Carl doesn't get to have his nasty little way with her. Even death is made to seem palatable, with a hip and irreverent medium (Whoopi Goldberg) on call to provide comic relief.

Ghost functions, variously, as a romantic fantasy, a comedy, a thriller and, naturally, a ghost story. But for all its attempts to assimilate as many mainstream conventions as possible – and its box-office returns would certainly indicate that it succeeded – the scene that has proved the most memorable[6] occurs while Sam is still in the land of the living. Narratively, it's the big romantic moment designed to render the subsequent tragedy all the more emotional. As Molly shapes clay at her pottery wheel, Sam sits behind her. He is shirtless. He puts his arms around her, placing his hands on top of hers, and they begin to shape the clay together; some of its damp consistency seeps through their fingers.

Apart from Sam's shirt, not a single item of clothing is removed, nor is a sexual organ on display. Physical contact between the lovers is minimal. These factors are reflected in the film's rating. Despite this, *Ghost* introduces a phallic symbol and then develops the metaphor by making it the tactile centre of the *mise en scène* for both participants. The suggestion is made, therefore, of mutual masturbation. The sludgy fluid that runs through their fingers as they manipulate the clay doubles for what pornographers call the 'money shot'.

Sex and the mainstream

The financial success of *Ghost* is indicative of the Hollywood mindset towards the blockbuster. As we have seen, the film incorporates elements of readily identifiable genres. The emphasis on tenderness and the non-explicit in its romantic scenes give it instant status as a 'chick flick'[7], while its thriller elements keep the male section of the audience placated. Comedic episodes detract from the fact that it deals with death (normally a box office turn-off). The non-occurrence of anything extreme, sexual or violent ensures a certificate conducive to a potentially larger audience.

The issue of whether children can gain admittance to a film is of great importance to studios. In the USA, films of an adult nature are often trimmed in order to secure them an NC-17 rating as opposed to an R rating. NC-17 denotes that children under 17 are permitted entry if accompanied by an adult. R, the equivalent of the British 18 certificate, is thought to compromise a film's chances at the box office; moreover, certain magazines refuse to carry advertising – crucial to public awareness of a new release – for R-rated movies.

Of course, there are many examples of films riding to box-office glory precisely *because* of controversy over their content, but even in such hyperbolic and widely reported cases as *Basic Instinct* (see chapter two), care was taken that an NC-17 was ultimately awarded to the film.

Two excellent examples of movies pitched at an adult audience, but non-explicit in their treatment of sexuality, can be found in the works of Stephen Soderbergh. In ***Sex, Lies and Videotape*** (1989) the eponymous tapes do not depict the act, but contain footage of various interviewees discussing their thoughts on, and experiences of, sex. Such is the hobby of Graham Walton (James Spader) – 'my personal project', as he calls it. Graham's project is the catalyst for a series of revelations, wherein the other elements of the title – the sex and the lies – are brought very much to the fore, without the director ever resorting to explicit imagery (indeed, the 18 rating imposed by the British Board of Film Classification (BBFC) can only owe to the very presence of the word 'sex' in the title).

Graham enters the film as a guest of his school friend John Millaney (Peter Gallagher), who he has not seen for nine years. John is a successful lawyer, driven by greed and egomania. Graham is a drifter, living out of his car and one suitcase. Time has left them with little in common, and Graham, not liking what John has become, drifts into a friendship with his wife, Ann (Andie MacDowell). Eventually, Ann becomes the subject of one of his tapes, as does Ann's sister, Cynthia (Laura San Giacomo), with whom John is having an affair.

If the videotapes Graham makes of the sisters stand as accusation against John, then Graham himself is no less challenged by Ann as regards his motives. Early on, he admits to her that he is impotent ('I can't get an erection in the presence of another person'). His tapes, therefore, are an emotional stand-in. One could almost say a replacement sex life, only he doesn't even use them as an aid to masturbation, but as a means of torturing himself over his inability to relate or communicate.

Soderbergh sets out his main themes in an opening sequence, which precedes Graham's arrival. Ann discusses with her therapist her concerns about having Graham as a guest in her house. He asks how things are between her and John.

> **Ann:** Last week I got this really strange feeling that I didn't want him to touch me.
> **Therapist:** Prior to this feeling, were you happy with your physical contact with John?
> **Ann:** Yeah. Except for, well, I've never really been that much into sex. I like it and everything, you know, but I don't think it's such a big deal … But lately I've just been kinda curious about how things have slacked off.

> **Therapist:** Perhaps he senses your hesitancy to be touched.
>
> **Ann:** But you see, that's the thing. He started not touching me before I started feeling like that.

The entire conversation takes place in voice-over, accompanied by scenes of John showing up at Cynthia's house, giving her a plant he has bought as a present, embracing her from behind and sliding a hand along her leg (she is wearing the indispensable little black dress); then he picks her up, Cynthia wrapping her legs around him, and carries her to the bed. Not only does this sequence sketch in the characters' interrelationships, acting as a sort of overture to the rest of the film, but the therapist's questions prefigure Graham's dispassionate interviewing style. Indeed, Graham's library of videotapes serves as a metaphor for middle-class America's obsession with therapy and self-unburdenment.

Out of Sight (1997), adapted from Elmore Leonard's novel, while firmly rooted in the thriller genre, is every bit the equal of _Sex, Lies and Videotape_ in terms of sophistication. The basic plot has convicted bank robber Jack Foley (George Clooney) kidnap Federal Marshal Karen Cisco (Jennifer Lopez) during a prison breakout. This is the beginning of a cat-and-mouse game that owes as much to their mutual attraction as to Karen's stated intent to recapture Jack. While investigating a gang of violent criminals Jack has reluctantly become involved with, Karen finds herself travelling between Miami and Detroit. Checking into a hotel populated by sales reps, all of whose advances she spurns, she is surprised by Jack's appearance.

The ensuing scene, in the hands of a journeyman director, could so easily have been mishandled. With its bland hotel rooms, romantic interlude between cop and fugitive, and the hard-edged criminal underworld scenes which bookend it, it could have been just a redundant sex scene included for the purposes of titillation before the gunplay of the finale. Soderbergh, however, turns it into an artful and tender love scene. He is well served by Scott Frank's screenplay, his dialogue as elegant as Soderbergh's direction.

The hotel interiors are turned into a romantic setting, the camera framing almost every shot against a window so that the lights of the city, seen through a silent fall of snow, provide a backdrop that is nocturnal, peaceful – almost timeless. This image is played upon throughout the scene; indeed, Jack is introduced in reflection as Karen gazes out into the night. Their conversation is witty and engaging.

Adding to the sense that the rest of the film's narrative concerns (i.e. its crime/thriller elements) have been put temporarily on hold, Jack and Karen adopt other identities as they flirt, calling each other Gary and Celeste. These alter egos are discarded as their behaviour becomes more tactile and their conversation more intimate. Editing paces the scene so that they are seen to draw closer even as they discuss the ephemerality of their relationship: dialogue continues in voice-over as Jack and Karen share moments where their communication is purely non-verbal.

Poster art for *Out of Sight* emphasizes its romantic thriller credentials.

The scene hinges on Jack's motivations in placing himself in a position where he could be arrested and re-incarcerated, and his confidence that Karen will not pursue this option.

> **Jack:** It's like seeing someone for the first time. You could be passing on the street and look at each other and for a few seconds there's this kind of recognition ... Next moment, the person's gone and it's too late to do anything about it. And you always remember it because it was there and you let it go. And you think to yourself, what if I had stopped, what if I had said something, what if? It may only happen a few times in your life.
> **Karen:** Or once.
> **Jack:** Or once.

As the scene progresses to their act of consummation, Soderbergh maintains the atmosphere of romanticism (there is a very gentle eroticism to the scene as well), without ever letting things become prurient. When the couple undress before each other, nudity is

27

avoided; as they begin to make love, a freeze-frame captures their intimacy, stopping short of the explicit.

Among the many pleasures *Out of Sight* offers is its sheer elegance: while never sacrificing its appeal to contemporary audiences (a neat bit of casting – Michael Keaton as jittery FBI operative Ray Nicolet – provides a link to Tarantino's *Jackie Brown*), it is directed with a panache pleasingly reminiscent of old-school Hollywood romantic thrillers.

A couple of classic Hitchcocks come to mind. **Rear Window** (1954) centres around photojournalist L B Jeffries (James Stewart), laid up in his Greenwich Village apartment after an accident has left him with a broken leg. Bored and increasingly tetchy, he occupies his days watching the comings and goings in the courtyard below and the apartments opposite, and his evenings bickering with his fiancée, society girl Lisa Fremont (Grace Kelly), who wants him to relinquish his dangerous assignments and become a portrait photographer. His broken leg serves as a metaphor for the sense of impotence that pervades their relationship (a commitment-phobe, he frets that Lisa is 'too perfect'). It is also the quintessential 'McGuffin' that sets in motion the plot: his enforced witnessing of a series of strange occurrences in one of the adjacent apartments, which suggests that the occupant may have murdered his wife. Confined to one spot, Jeffries's viewpoint becomes the audience's viewpoint. Therefore, everything is rendered subjective and the audience becomes complicit in his voyeurism.

Hitchcock's subtle achievement is that he incorporates the psychological darkness of his later works (see chapters four and five for analyses of, respectively, *Marnie* and *Vertigo*) into one of his most mainstream and fondly remembered films. Not only does Jeffries become obsessive in his scoptophilia – this is, after all, a man who has spent his life framing his subjects through the lens of a camera: the window of his apartment thus becomes a substitute – but he projects his obsession onto two other people, Lisa and his nurse Stella (Thelma Ritter), whom he beguiles into carrying out his amateur attempts at detective work.

For a film that is therefore not just about, but an exercise in, voyeurism there is nothing in terms of explicit content. There is, in fact, a cleanliness to *Rear Window* that is surprisingly endearing; even the chemistry between Stewart and the never more effervescent Grace Kelly is more elegant than erotic. Even when she agrees to spend the night at his apartment ('but I've only got one bed'), Jeffries still can't keep his mind off the 'case'. As she unpacks her nightdress, he ruminates about which of his neighbours he's going to pay closest attention to next.

> **Lisa:** Not if I have to move into an apartment across the way [she begins drawing down the blinds] and do the dance of the seven veils every hour. Show's over for tonight. [She indicates the nightdress.] Preview of coming attractions. [Moments later, she re-appears, radiant in diaphanous white.] What do you think?
> **Jeffries** (breathtaken): Well, I …
> **Lisa:** I'll rephrase the question. Do you like it?

It's clear he does, but before he can do anything about it, a scream resounds from the courtyard and Hitchcock steers his audience away from the brief possibility of sex, and back to the safer business of murder.

North by Northwest (1959) has all the mainstream appeal of *Rear Window*, as well as the same suave, ironic approach to its darker aspects. The narrative is secondary (Hitchcock apparently instructed Ernest Lehman that he wanted, amongst other set-pieces, a murder in the United Nations building and a cliffhanger finale on Mount Rushmore, and left the screenwriter to thread these iconic moments together); Hitchcock is more interested in immersing his bemused hero, Roger Thornhill (Cary Grant), in a Freudian nightmare. Challenges to his identity (and by extension, his sexual self-identity) are made manifest from the word go. Mistaken for an undercover agent, he is menaced by master criminal Phillip Vandamm (James Mason) and his decidedly effete henchman Leonard (Martin Landau). Set up for a murder he didn't commit, he goes on the run from both the police and a shadowy security agency headed by The Professor (Leo G Carroll). All the while, he is hindered and gently mocked by his ageing but thoroughly stubborn mother, Clara (Jessie Royce Landis).

In terms of the film's subtext, Vandamm and Leonard represent

Travelling companions: Cary Grant and Eva Marie Saint in Hitchcock's *North by Northwest.*

a homosexual threat; the murder and pursuit imply impotence (he tries to convince the authorities of his innocence and of Vandamm's part in the events, but can present no evidence in his favour and is thus disbelieved); and Clara's continual hindrance/possessiveness is the most cynical portrayal of the mother figure in Hitchcock's filmography this side of a certain Mrs Bates.

Of course, this being Hitch, there has to be a drop-dead gorgeous blonde mixed up in it somewhere. Step forward Eve Kendall (Eva Marie Saint) who, while in the pay of Vandamm, dupes Thornhill into believing she is acting in his best interests. She earns his trust by helping him escape his pursuers and smuggling him onboard a cross-continental train. In the privacy of their compartment, they discuss the case – then each other. Revisiting a ploy he had used to get *Notorious* past the censors in 1946 (when even the length of time two characters could kiss was carefully monitored), Hitchcock intersperses their dialogue with extended bouts of smooching and running of hands through hair. He also uses the motion of the train to jolt them together; as they make their way from the door of the compartment to the couchette, he has them pivot before the camera (the composition never alters). It's a clever touch, an inversion of the standard romantic scene where the hero and heroine retain their position while the camera whirls dervishly around them. It also sets up the heavily Freudian closing shot where Thornhill, having proved his masculinity by defeating the bad guys and getting the girl, embarks on another railway journey with Eve. Hitchcock cuts from the two of them climbing into their bunk together to the train disappearing into a tunnel.

As obvious as this kind of imagery is, it reinforces the fact that both *Rear Window* and *North by Northwest*, given the prevailing censorial climate of the times, had to hide their cynical psychological undercurrents beneath a veneer of slick, romantic entertainment. *Out of Sight*, made almost 40 years down the line, did not have to be so coy; many 15-rated films of the last decade or so have delivered scenes of notable sexual content[8]. Indeed, as critical as the issue of certification is, sex has always had its place in mainstream film production.

Claude Lelouch's **Un Homme et Une Femme** (1966) – made a decade after the Hitchcock films discussed above – has the same cleanliness to its depiction of sexuality as *Rear Window*; unsurprisingly, perhaps, since this is, after all, a film about a love affair which was awarded a commendation by the Catholic Church. The manner in which lovers-to-be Jean-Louis Duroc (Jean-Louis Trintignant) and Anne Gauthier (Anouk Aimée) meet sets the tone: their children attend the same school. In their late-thirties and with previous marriages behind them, both are still impossibly photogenic. Both have glamorous jobs (he's a racing driver, she works in film production). And both are nursing the loss of their erstwhile spouses. Anne's stuntman husband died in an accident on-set. Jean-Louis's wife, while he was comatose following a crash on the track, suffered a nervous breakdown and committed suicide.

Three-quarters of the film's running time is devoted to the gradual development of feelings between them. They spend time together in picturesque locations. Their children (his son and her daughter) play together. Lelouch's camera lingers on sunsets, swans gliding across lakes, golden beaches and sailboats out at sea. The patterns of light on water are endlessly poeticized. Lelouch prettifies every element, just as Bo Widerberg would do a year later in *Elvira Madigan*. Postponement of Jean-Louis and Anne's consummation until the closing stages of the film also marks *Un Homme et Une Femme* as a precursor of *Summer of '42* (Robert Mulligan, 1971), where everything is a soft-focus prelude to a not particularly explicit (or even erotic) payoff in the last few minutes.

Lelouch's love scene alternates between black-and-white and colour, as Anne is tormented by memories of her husband, even while she and Jean-Louis share their most intimate moments. Not that Lelouch deviates from head-and-shoulders close-ups of the lovers; nor do their kisses ever become too passionate, or their hands rove anywhere other than each other's face. Interestingly, Lelouch films their lovemaking in black-and-white and opts for colour whenever the flashbacks intrude. The effect is to heighten Anne's sense of guilt at what she perceives as a betrayal of her husband's memory.

Un Homme et Une Femme is notable for the introduction of emotional complexities into the kind of scene which many films depict on a purely physical level. Its visual style and dreamy soft-focus mark it as very much a product of its times, and it makes for interesting comparison to the works of, say, Bertrand Blier, who emerged a decade later and challenged cinematic and social conventions (see chapter three).

But of course, filmmaking, as much as any other art form, evolves by adapting to changing social mores. Mainstream cinema, though, has always flourished by working within parameters defined by that which is popular – and as much, maybe more so, by that which is acceptable.

An interesting aesthetic comparison can be gained from considering two sets of originals and their respective remakes, one that functions, like *Out of Sight*, as a romantic thriller; and one that generated as much controversy in 1997 as its original incarnation did in 1961.

The Thomas Crown Affair (Norman Jewison, 1968), is very much a product of its time: chic, glossy and burdened with an overuse of what was then a newly pioneered cinematic technique – split-screen. Still, its popularity was spectacular; likewise that of its title song, 'The Windmills of Your Mind'. Unconventionally, Jewison gets the thriller elements out of the way right at the start, with successful businessman and inveterate playboy Crown (Steve McQueen) planning and executing a bank robbery for no other reason than to prove he can do it. Thereafter, the romantic narrative is brought to the fore as insurance investigator Vicky Anderson (Faye Dunaway) closes in on him. As with Karen Cisco, professional obligations become clouded as her attraction to him develops.

The key scene – in which their battle of wits takes on a more sexual aspect – is staged, appropriately enough, over a game. Thomas and Vicky face each other across a chessboard. The camera circles them (just as they have been circling each other). Both are dressed as if for a romantic meal, he very suave in an immaculate suit, she looking like the proverbial million dollars in a backless dress with plunging neckline. This is not the only distraction Crown has to contend with; in a visual metaphor as unsubtle – and suggestive of masturbation – as that in *Ghost*, Vicky spends most of the game running her fingers along the length and over the tip of a chess piece (the bishop – make of that what you will!).

John McTiernan's ***The Thomas Crown Affair*** (1999) retains the idea of criminal endeavours (and the legal and financial consequences thereof) being nothing more to its protagonists than a game – 'only important to very silly rich people' as McCann (Dennis Leary), the detective assigned to work with the insurance investigator, puts it – but leaves out the chess match.

There are other changes: Crown (Pierce Brosnan) is now an art thief with a passion for Monet; his role in the heist is proactive (in the original, he masterminds it but doesn't participate); and the ending is unashamedly crowd-pleasing, with Crown and Catherine Banning (Rene Russo) – such is the insurance agent renamed – ending up together (as opposed to the final double-cross on which they part in Jewison's film). Likewise, the scene in which Crown and Catherine quit circling each other and get down to business is staged quite differently. The scene is a society ball; Crown is in attendance, accompanied by a young super-model type. As they glide almost demurely across the dance floor, a tap on Crown's shoulder interrupts the proceedings. Catherine, a knockout by anyone's standards in a clinging black number and red sash, has gatecrashed the party and is cutting in.

Crown's companion disappears, notably peeved. The band jazz things up with a rumba. Movements on the dance floor become funkier, sexier and infinitely more suggestive. And there's no doubt Catherine is the centre of attention. The effect of this scene is similar to the music and dance sequences

The chessboard as a metaphor for seduction in *The Thomas Crown Affair.*

already discussed in *The Fabulous Baker Boys, From Dusk Till Dawn* et al: everything stops to acknowledge the centrality of the female figure. Catherine's dance with Crown is a sexual challenge, one he answers when he pulls her to him and asks, 'Do you wanna dance, or do you wanna dance?'

McTiernan effects a stylish segue here, as an overhead shot of Crown and Banning embracing amidst a melange of circling couples is replaced by an overhead shot of the foyer to Crown's elegantly appointed townhouse, he and Catherine still whirling in their own private dance. This in turn is superseded by a montage of the couple, clothes and inhibitions equally shed, doing the proverbial wild thing in as many locations as chez Crown has to offer: the hallway, the stairs, the desk of Crown's office.

Notably, for all that the earlier scenes of the film (and the whole of Jewison's original) revolve around the balance of power between the gentleman thief and the sophisticated insurance agent, it is in this love scene that McTiernan abandons this aspect of things and allows them consummation of their mutual attraction as equals.

The two film versions of Vladimir Nabokov's novel *Lolita* are likewise separated by three decades, which lends a more explicit tone to the proceedings in the remake. But the subject matter is something altogether different. A romantic thriller it is not. There can be no hedging the issue: *Lolita* (in whichever form one approaches it) is about the love of a middle-aged man for an underage girl. The novel was published in 1955 to universal controversy. Elegantly written and steeped in the wit and wordplay for which Nabokov was famous, it is a meditation on love, desire and loss of innocence – except that these concepts are examined in the context of their least socially acceptable manifestation.

Both adaptations do not deviate from the basic story: Professor Humbert Humbert (James Mason in the original, Jeremy Irons in the remake) accepts a teaching post in a quiet American town. He takes lodgings at the house of Charlotte Haze (Shelley Winters/Melanie Griffith), a blowsy widow who becomes attracted to him. Although the feeling is resolutely not mutual, Humbert enters into marriage with her. His decision is motivated by the idea that it will put him closer to Charlotte's daughter Dolores, nicknamed Lolita (Sue Lyon/Dominique Swain), with whom he has fallen in love. When Charlotte sends Lolita to summer camp, Humbert despairs. Shortly afterwards, Charlotte flees the house after discovering Humbert's diary wherein he describes his detestation of her and his feelings for Lolita. She is hit by a car and killed. Humbert, now Lolita's legal guardian, takes her on a trip across America, during which their

The nymphet as icon: Sue Lyon in Kubrick's *Lolita*.

relationship develops. They are, however, being shadowed by Clare Quilty (Peter Sellers/Frank Langella), a dissipated writer and fellow paedophile ('another like me' as Humbert finally admits), who has his own designs on her.

Stanley Kubrick's **Lolita** (1961) was scripted by the author, something which perhaps works to its detriment. As significant a cinematic achievement as anything bearing Kubrick's name, it remains overlong, with many scenes weighted by superfluous characters and dialogue. Nonetheless, Kubrick's direction has a cool elegance, which accommodates Nabokov's sense of satire.

Adrian Lyne's **Lolita** (1997) is a shorter, more tightly constructed film, and also manages to reinstate Nabokov's prelude, crucial to understanding his anti-hero's psychology, where the youthful Humbert loses his first love, the 14-year-old Annabel, to typhus. 'The child I loved was gone,' he opines in voice-over, 'but I kept looking for her, long after I left my own childhood behind. The poison was in the wound, you see, and the wound wouldn't heal.' This admission, just minutes in, that there is something very wrong with Humbert's world view, is poles apart from Kubrick's very discreet treatment where the main theme had, by its very nature, to be unspoken – absolutely implicit – in order that the film ever see the inside of a cinema. (It is worth noting that both films advance Lolita's age to her mid-teens; in the novel, she is just 12.)

Three examples, all similarly staged, differentiate the film-makers' approach to the material. Firstly, the introduction of Lolita herself. Kubrick has her lounging in the garden, propped up on one arm, reading a movie magazine. She is wearing a two-piece bathing suit, an outsized sun-hat and dark glasses, over the

Advertising for Adrian Lyne's remake: the key image of Kubrick's film revisited.

JEREMY
IRONS

MELANIE
GRIFFITH

FRANK
LANGELLA

"Best film so far this year."

Hugo Williams - HARPERS & QUEEN

Lolita

18

top of which she peers knowingly at Humbert, recognizing from the outset that he covets her. Lyne retains the setting, but introduces a sprinkler, jetting water across the verdant lawn as it moves through its 360-degree rotation. Lolita is lying on her stomach, upper body raised on her arms as she peruses the magazine. Quite why her reading matter hasn't turned into papier mâché is unexplained, since Lolita herself has received a comprehensive soaking, her pale sundress clinging to every contour of her body.

Secondly, Lolita's leave-taking before her enforced summer camp exile. In the original, having been bundled into the car by her mother, she runs back into the house. Here, Humbert is waiting for her. 'Don't forget me,' she says, then reluctantly turns and leaves. In the remake, she throws herself upon Humbert, kissing him full on the lips while his hand lingers on the bare skin revealed by her backless top.

Thirdly, the moment of Lolita's complicity, which occurs after Humbert has picked her up from summer camp, but before he tells her of Charlotte's death. They stay overnight at a motel. The following morning, having spent an uncomfortable night on a campbed at the foot of Lolita's bed, Humbert is awakened by her.

> **Lolita:** Well, what shall we do now?
> **Humbert:** We should ring down and order breakfast.
> **Lolita:** I don't want to do that.
> **Humbert:** Well, what do you want to do?
> **Lolita:** Why don't we play a game? ... I learned some real good games in camp. One in particular was fun ... I played it with Charlie.
> **Humbert:** A boy? You and he?
> **Lolita:** Are you sure you can't guess what the game was?
> **Humbert:** I'm not really a very good guesser.

Lolita leans over and whispers in his ear, hand cupped round her mouth. Then she straightens up, giggling.

> **Lolita:** You never played that game when you were a kid?
> **Humbert:** No, never.
> **Lolita:** All right, then.

At which point Kubrick fades to black. Lyne makes the point a little more directly. Not only do Humbert and Lolita share the same bed in the motel; when they wake, she begins kissing him on the mouth before a word has even been said. Then, and only then, does she whisper her confession in his ear.

> **Humbert:** You played that game with Charlie at camp?
> **Lolita:** Don't tell me you never tried it when you were a kid?
> **Humbert:** No, never.
> **Lolita:** I guess I'm going to have to show you everything.

She straddles him and unties the drawstring around his pyjamas. A close-up of Humbert's face shows him in raptures. This is the point at which Lyne fades out, but even then, he has Humbert add in voice-over, 'Gentlewomen of the jury, I was not even her first lover.'

The scene that most effectively demonstrates the aesthetic disparity of the two films, however, is Humbert and Lolita's argument over her appearance in a play (scripted by Quilty). The dynamic of the scene is Humbert's sexual jealousy and need to control Lolita. Kubrick relies solely on dialogue; the conversation is conducted while Humbert gives her a pedicure.

> **Humbert:** I thought we understood no dates ... I don't want you around nasty-minded boys.
> **Lolita:** Oh, you're a fine one to talk about somebody else's mind ... You never let me have any fun.
> **Humbert:** Fun? You have all the fun in the world. If you want anything, I buy it for you immediately ... You and I, we have lots of fun, don't we Lolita?
> **Lolita:** Come here. [He goes and sits on the other side of the bed.] Still love me?
> **Humbert:** Completely. You know that.
> **Lolita:** I want you to be proud of me. Really proud of me. You see, they want me for the lead in the school play.

Kubrick plays the rest of the scene in a similar vein: a lover's tiff, with Humbert unable to stop being jealous and possessive, scared Lolita will get too close to other people and the truth about them be discovered. Lyne does things differently.

> **Lolita:** I'm supposed to be in a play.
> **Humbert:** With the boys from Butler's Academy? ... I don't think it's a good idea.

She sits on the floor in front of him and uses one foot (the camera lingers on her painted toenails) to push his rocking chair (a significant metaphor on their age differences). She then uses her foot to caress his upper thigh and groin.

> **Lolita:** Like that? You want more, don't you? … I think it should be two dollars.
> **Humbert:** Dollar fifty.
> **Lolita:** I really do think it should be two dollars. [She sits up and uses her hand to caress him.] Am I right?
> **Humbert:** God, yes. Two dollars.
> **Lolita:** And I should be in the play.

A subsequent scene – startling for being the only time Lyne has his protagonists fully naked – has them squabbling over money, coins cast onto rumpled sheets, Humbert whining 'You can't expect me to pay extra in the middle' as Lolita twists her lithe young body away from him.

As these comparisons demonstrate, Kubrick's film relies upon suggestiveness to convince the audience they have seen, or been party to, more than has actually been portrayed on screen. As noted earlier, this approach was, of course, necessitated by the censorial climate of the times. The fact remains, however, that when implicit material is used well, cinema is capable of exerting an undeniable power of almost subconscious arousal.

explicit

CHAPTER TWO

A s the differences between the two versions of *Lolita* prove, the very nature of what is considered challenging or risqué alters from generation to generation and is redefined from decade to decade. Often, a contentious film can be seen to use the very sexual aspects that make it controversial as something of a patina beneath which a deeper social or aesthetic point is made.

Take Alain Resnais's ***Hiroshima, Mon Amour*** (1959). At the time of its release, it attracted a huge mainstream audience because of its frank depiction of sexual expression. Nonetheless, it is an art film through and through. Its dissonant narrative, which incorporates flashbacks as well as flash-forwards (a device Resnais returns to throughout his filmography), is interwoven with documentary footage. There are large amounts of voice-over dialogue, which range from the profound to the ambiguous. Lengthy tracking shots through the eponymous city enhance a sense of discontinuity.

Such story as Resnais offers centres around a French woman (Emmanuelle Riva), visiting Hiroshima to participate in a film about the aftermath of the atomic bombs which levelled the city at the end of the Second World War, and the Japanese man, an architect[1], she enters into an affair with (Eiji Okada). Neither character is named; throughout the film, they refer to each other as Nevers and Hiroshima, their respective home towns. The French woman reveals how, as a younger woman, she had an affair with a German soldier while Nevers was occupied, an act for which she was punished by the townspeople. Their connection is through experiences forged during the war.

Resnais presents a synthesis of the themes that run through the film from the very first scene, as well as focusing on the shape and form of the naked human body. In a tableau that seems caught outside of time – it could be a prelude to intercourse, or a moment of shared tenderness afterwards – the couple hold each other as first ash, then rain, gusts across their skin. The ash is obviously a reference to the destruction of Hiroshima, while the rain symbolizes cleansing and purification. And in the nudity, much fêted in its time, in the physical contact – the intimacy – between two people of different races and cultures lies the hope and humanity of the film.

Sex and silence: the explicit and the existential

It is open to conjecture whether the cross-racial element of the relationship depicted in *Hiroshima, Mon Amour* was as much a factor in the controversy it generated (and the audience it gained) as the nudity on display. Certainly, it raised the curtain on a number of key European and arthouse films which would garner headlines and outrage the moral majority over the subsequent decades. If the nature of the couple's relationship in Resnais's film can be described as existential – and there can be little doubt that, for the period of time they spend together, they are the only thing in each other's life – then this sense of emotional, or more often than not sexual, communion as a raison d'être is as explicit in the following examples as the onscreen excesses which illustrate the point.

Blow-Up (Michelangelo Antonioni, 1966) is a veritable treatise on the emptiness of modern life, in which sex (for all that it is offered, used and discarded with chic indifference) is the only alternative to an all-pervading malaise. The absence of meaning in the life of protagonist Thomas (David Hemmings) is illustrated by his profession, and expounded in the pretence of plot that informs the film. A fashion/glamour photographer who is more famous than any of the women he shoots, his high opinion of himself is clear by the way he treats his models: he refers to them as 'birds', and arranges them like plastic dolls into vacuous tableaux. 'On your back,' he curtly instructs one of them, straddling her as he snaps pictures.

An indication of Thomas's emotional hollowness is the act he commits by which the 'plot' is set in motion. After a visit to an antiques shop for props for his next shoot, he wanders through a public park, snapping off a few shots as he walks. Seeing a courting couple, he adopts a more furtive approach, hiding as he finishes the roll of film.

Having developed the photographs and made enlargements, he realizes the woman, Jane (Vanessa Redgrave), is looking at something in the undergrowth, her face registering horror. He produces blow-ups of key areas of the negative – the image losing definition the more extreme these enlargements become. He sees enough – the shadowy outline of someone holding a gun; what looks like a body behind a fence – to surmise that a murder has occurred. The mystery seems to give him a purpose hitherto missing in his life, but it is one he is unable to solve: the closer he looks, the further the image retracts.

It is through this element of the film that Antonioni passes comment on (a) the old adage that the camera never lies and (b) the sterility of images that have no meaning behind them (Thomas's deepening obsession with what is hidden in the photograph is continually contrasted with the superfluity of his fashion/glamour work). Antonioni's critique also extends to the 'free love' ethos of the Swinging Sixties. When Jane asks Thomas for the pictures back, he feigns indifference until she finally offers him sexual favours. In return, he gives her an unexposed roll of film. Later, in the film's most controversial scene (which gave UK cinema-goers their first mainstream glimpse of pubic hair), he cajoles two naive models into a threesome. Impolite to them from the moment they arrive at his studio ('put the kettle on,' he snaps; 'you can make a cup of coffee, can't you?'), he bursts in on them unannounced while they are changing, sexually harasses them, then hustles them into his studio, partially disrobed. Some element of pre-existing sexual tension between the models comes to the fore and their behaviour veers into a scene of borderline lesbianism. This provides sufficient affront to Thomas's masculinity for him to join in, swiftly establishing himself as the dominant party. Afterwards, he throws them out (when they protest that he hasn't photographed them, he tersely replies, 'I'm too whacked, it's your own fault') and goes back to the picture he has become obsessed by: the mystery he can never solve.

Another decade, another dissection of social malcontent – and the Seventies, a decade like no other in terms of controversial, hard-hitting films[2] offers plenty of scope. As with Antonioni, it was a European filmmaker directing a mainstream actor who challenged the sensibilities of the cinema-going public. Bernardo Bertolucci's **Last Tango in Paris** (1972) stars Marlon Brando as Paul, an ex-patriate American whose Paris-based lifestyle has begun to disintegrate since the suicide of his wife (who, as he discovers during the course of the film, had been having an affair). He meets a considerably younger woman, Jeanne (Maria Schneider) – he is in late middle-age; she is just twenty – while she is searching for an apartment to move into with Tom (Jean-Pierre Leaud), her documentary-maker boyfriend. He wants to make a film exploring the truth of their relationship. She responds by athletically entering into a purely sexual relationship with Paul, who establishes the nature of their liaisons from the outset: 'You and I are going to meet here and forget everything that goes on outside here. We are going to forget everything we knew. Everything.'

It is tempting to interpret her cuckolding of an earnest young artistic type with a shambolic and overweight older man as a comment on the need for a director to whore himself to an audience who respond to a film's sexual content rather than its artistic concerns. One can almost say that Bertolucci presupposes this necessity, hence the butter scene. Unlike *Blow-Up*, which is built around an enigma, a half-image that will never reveal the truth, what takes place in *Last Tango in Paris* is absolute. When Paul pins Jeanne face down to the floor, forces himself on top of her and uses butter as lubricant to effect anal intercourse, the act defines itself. It is a shatteringly nihilistic moment, which almost provides an emotional full stop to a film that still has an hour's running time left.

What it achieves, though, is to throw into greater disparity the differences between Paul and Tom. If Tom is driven by a sense of creative integrity, using film as a search for the truth, then Paul's motivation is utterly basic: oblivion through sex. Given that

Sex and death: Eiko Matsuda and Tatsuya Fuji take it to the limit in *Ai No Corrida*.

Jeanne emerges as little more than an object, one is left with the impression that Bertolucci vacillates between the two male characters in terms of empathy, constantly questioning the roles of both director and protagonist.

Released just four years after *Last Tango in Paris*, Nagisa Oshima's **Ai No Corrida** (*In the Realm of the Senses*, 1976) took the theme of emotional malaise and sexual obsession to its extreme. Unlike *Blow-Up* and *Last Tango in Paris*, it was not contemporarily set (both of these earlier films are very much a comment on the cultural zeitgeist of their respective times and places). *Ai No Corrida* takes place in 1936, and is based on a widely reported case from that year when a woman was discovered walking through Tokyo clutching the severed penis of her dead lover. Oshima's film is a fictive document of the events leading up to this point.

When ex-prostitute Sada (Eiko Matsuda) seeks employment at the house of Kichizo (Tatsuya Fuji), a priapic but otherwise respectable businessman, they are soon embroiled in an affair as solely motivated by the physical as that of Paul and Jeanne. Most of the film's running time consists of Sada and Kichizo having sex. Oshima challenges audience sensibilities by including scenes of fellatio and penetration. Images proliferate which, while hardly arousing, can justly be considered hardcore: Sada fellates Kichizo while he coolly smokes a cigarette; ejaculate runs from her mouth as she raises her head from his penis; later, unable to have intercourse because of Sada's period, Kichizo insists on masturbating her, his fingers slick with blood when he removes them; later still, Sada having returned to prostitution, he takes her from behind before she leaves to visit a client – then, when their housekeeper (advanced in years and overweight) remonstrates with him about his lifestyle, he throws up her skirt and takes her the same way. A similar scene of sexual violence has four geishas watch Sada and Kichizo's exertions. When one professes to be shocked, the others hold her down and penetrate her with a wooden dildo.

Elsewhere, the food/sex correlation (used as metaphor in *Spartacus* and *Tom Jones*) is present and correct. They have intercourse while dining, Kichizo seasoning his sushi in Sada's vagina. This course finished, he turns his attention to a hardboiled egg, which he inserts into her. He eats it whole when she returns it.

Their relationship moves beyond the obsessive, to the masochistic. Kichizo responds excitedly to Sada hitting him during sex. When he cuts himself shaving, she licks the blood from his cheek. During an argument over whether he is still seeing his wife, she inflicts bite-wounds on him. As the film nears its almost unwatchable conclusion, they resort to erotic asphyxiation. Kichizo cannot bring himself to perform the act of strangulation, but insists Sada do so on him. Which she does – more than willingly.

Practitioners of erotic asphyxiation, one of the most dangerous areas of sexual experimentation, experience heightened sexual gratification as a result of bringing themselves to the verge of asphyxiation. It is often, when a part of solitary sexual behaviour (when it is known as autoerotic asphyxiation), the cause of 'accidental' suicides. With Sada and Kichizo, it represents something of a sadomasochistic endgame. Kichizo has already acceded power to Sada (the red silk scarf she uses to choke him with is very redolent of bondage, another example of sexual power games); now she uses it in an act of horrible finality. After a protracted session of sex with asphyxiation, during which Sada almost kills Kichizo, he drifts into unconsciousness, unable to satisfy her any more. Sada crosses the line from obsession to madness. Straddling him, she strangles him while he sleeps. Waking the next morning to the realization of what she has done, she takes a knife to his flaccid penis, then stumbles out in the streets, his dismemberment clutched in her hands.

Madness as a result of sexual obsession is also charted in **Betty Blue** (Jean-Jacques Beineix, 1986), but here it culminates in the death of the emotionally unstable heroine and not her lover. The opening scene, one of cinema's most celebrated onscreen acts of sex, sets the tone. A single take clocking in at two minutes, it begins in long shot, Zorg (Jean-Hughes Anglade) and Betty (Béatrice Dalle) coupling enthusiastically. Slowly, the camera moves towards them, so that by the time their joint orgasm has been reached, they are framed in close-up. Spent, they lie gasping for breath. 'I had known Betty for a week,' Zorg intones in voice-over. 'We screwed every night. A thunderstorm was coming.'

Some thunderstorm. As the film progresses, Betty forcibly drags Zorg, a handyman living an unassuming life having given up on his youthful ambitions of being a writer, out of the rut he has wilfully allowed himself to settle into. Discovering his dog-eared old manuscripts, she harangues him into writing again, compelling him to leave his shabby old cabin by the coast (she takes the rather extreme measure of burning it down) and travel across France in order to experience life, to glean the material for the great novel of which she believes him capable.

She gives him love, inspiration, excitement – even danger – but at a terrible cost to herself. Not the most rational of individuals to begin with, her relationship with Zorg grows increasingly possessive. Their arguments become as passionate and violent as their lovemaking, as a result of which Betty perpetrates acts of self-harm. Zorg gets involved in a series of misadventures, culminating in his participation in an armed robbery. Essentially, he begins living his novel instead of writing it.

Betty is hospitalized following a nervous breakdown. Rather than allow the shock therapy the doctors advocate, Zorg resorts to euthanasia, smothering her with a pillow. There is a horrible sense of completeness in his actions: the film begins with an act of sex and ends with one of death. The opening scene has Betty and Zorg abandoning themselves to each other. The rest of the film is a gradual abandonment of everything, until only one of them is left.

As bleak as the ending of *Betty Blue* is (even though Zorg's novel is eventually published, the success Betty has driven him towards comes too late to save her), it's a colourful little fable compared to

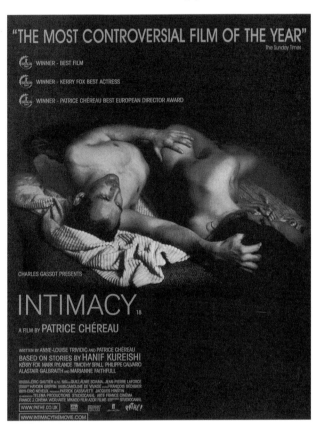

"THE MOST CONTROVERSIAL FILM OF THE YEAR"
The Sunday Times

WINNER - BEST FILM

WINNER - KERRY FOX BEST ACTRESS

WINNER - PATRICE CHÉREAU BEST EUROPEAN DIRECTOR AWARD

CHARLES GASSOT PRESENTS

INTIMACY 18

A FILM BY PATRICE CHÉREAU

WRITTEN BY ANNE-LOUISE TRIVIDIC AND PATRICE CHÉREAU
BASED ON STORIES BY HANIF KUREISHI
KERRY FOX MARK RYLANCE TIMOTHY SPALL PHILIPPE CALVARIO
ALASTAIR GALBRAITH AND MARIANNE FAITHFULL

ERIC GAUTIER A.F.C. GUILLAUME SCIAMA JEAN-PIERRE LAFORCE
HAYDEN GRIFFIN CAROLINE DE VIVAISE FRANÇOIS GÉDIGIER
ÉRIC NEVEUX PATRICK CASSAVETTI JACQUES HINSTIN
TELEMA PRODUCTIONS STUDIOCANAL ARTE FRANCE CINÉMA
FRANCE 2 CINÉMA WDR/ARTE MIKADO FILM AZOR FILMS STUDIOCANAL

WWW.PATHE.CO.UK   PATHÉ
WWW.INTIMACYTHEMOVIE.COM

Sex without glamour: poster art for *Intimacy* captures the film's aesthetic.

Intimacy (Patrice Chéreau, 2001). Set in London's dreariest locations, it is an examination of emotional apathy, wasted lives and sex as little more than a distraction. 'You're the least alive person I know,' Claire (Kerry Fox) screams at her husband at one point – and it's an accusation that can be levelled at the entire cast. Claire's dreams of establishing herself as an actress are manifested in the (bad) performances of Tennessee Williams she gives with an amateur group in a small theatre beneath a pub. Her taxi-driver husband, Andy (Timothy Spall), spends every free hour in the pub, desultorily playing pool and chivvying along the punters with assurances of how talented his wife is. Both are deluding themselves.

Every Wednesday afternoon, Claire visits a dingy flat belonging to divorced barman Jay (Mark Rylance). The walls are bare plaster, undecorated. The carpet is dotted with cigarette burns. The only warmth is from a one-bar electric fire propped in the corner. In this depressing environment, Claire and Jay conduct a wordless act of sex. This weekly meeting has become their routine. 'It's a drag,' Jay tells his co-worker Ian (Philippe Calvario), but when Claire does not appear one Wednesday afternoon, he mopes around the flat looking for all the world like a schoolboy who has been stood up on his first date.

In fact, Jay (for all that he is, nominally at least, the protagonist) is the biggest loser in the film. A decent-looking, educated, eloquent man, he seems almost wilfully to have wasted his life. He admits that his job is going nowhere, but he has held it down for six years. His solitary existence is of his own making, having walked out on his wife and two children for a reason he never fully justifies. Claire, on the other hand, is married, with a son, and at least has aspirations. It is when Jay starts taking an interest in Claire's life outside of their Wednesday afternoon arrangement that he betrays her as surely as he betrayed his own family.

Intimacy earned controversy on its release, as *Sight and Sound* put it, 'for [exposing] audiences … to what various British newspapers have stopwatched as 35 minutes of explicit screen sex, including the first brief shot of a serious actress fellating her co-star'[3]. This scene is possibly the most startling in the film. Although it is preceded by two graphic scenes of intercourse (Chéreau's camera unblinking in recording their coupling), on neither occasion does he move into the realm of what can be considered hardcore filmmaking by showing penetration. Here, however, he presents an image seldom found outside of pornography (except in, say, *Ai No Corrida*), and presents it in a way that is dispassionate, cold, unerotic. This approach typifies each of the sexual encounters in *Intimacy*: there is no romantic music on the soundtrack (no music at all, in fact, just the grunts and gasps of the couple); there is no soft-focus, flattering lighting, or artful composition to the cinematography; there is nothing graceful, langorous or sensuous about what takes place. Quite the opposite. It is real, just as the failed lives depicted in the film are, sadly, all too real.

Soft core: mainstream sex and the 'erotic thriller'

The films considered so far in this chapter have all used sexual imagery to make a point, be it political, social or aesthetic. And while they have been dogged by controversy (and, in cases like *Ai No Corrida* and *Intimacy*, labelled hardcore by the media), less worthy films have routinely been produced, films with just as great a degree of emphasis on sexual representation (in many instances, sexual objectification), but devoid of artistic merit.

Such fare has, of course, been around since the earliest days of the moving image. In her exhaustive study *Hard Core*, Linda Williams traces the roots of contemporary pornography back to stag films, i.e. cheaply made short films designed for a private, all-male audience. 'What the butler saw' machines – coin-fed devices containing a sequence of still photographs rotated by a handle to create the impression of movement – catered to a similar audience. While the actual content of these early examples is poles apart from pornography as the term is understood today (one might roughly define it as anything of an explicit sexual nature which is held to contain no artistic merit, and produced for no other reason than to arouse), there is little aesthetic difference. Both types of entertainment are aimed squarely at the libido. Their purpose is to titillate, to arouse; primarily, to provide material for masturbatory fantasies.

Likewise, mainstream cinema has not only exploited the requirements of such viewers, but cynically sought to bring in a wider audience by packaging its offerings in genres that are easy to categorize, interspersing its sexual *mise en scènes* with enough in the way of plot to affect a sense of cinematic legitimacy by dint of narrative development. Take, for instance, **Emmanuelle** (Just Jaeckin, 1974). Upon the slenderest of plots – a diplomat's wife travels with her husband to Bangkok, gets bored when he neglects her in favour of his work, and looks elsewhere for fulfilment – is hung a sequence of sexual encounters which, even as each strives to be different from that preceding it, become increasingly interminable.

Emmanuelle (Sylvia Kristel) runs a gamut of partners – male and female – as well as trying out many different locations: aircraft, opium dens, squash courts, massage parlours, swimming pools. Each encounter is interspersed with equally laborious faux-intellectual dialogue, expounding on sexual freedom as a means of self-discovery. This verbiage reaches its apogee when Emmanuelle meets Mario (Alain Cluny). A sensualist in late middle age, he compensates for his lost youth by orchestrating Emmanuelle's misadventures, telling her 'we have to make love without reason or restraint'. He exposes her (in both senses of the word) to drunken lechers and dope fiends, offering no protection when two addicts force themselves on her at the opium den. Later, he takes her to a back-street boxing venue where two brutish fighters engage in a kickboxing contest. As it ends, Mario laconically informs her that she is the winner's prize. Finally, Mario encourages her to participate in threesomes. 'Every act of love should include a third partner,' he pontificates. Of course, it is Mario himself who makes up the numbers. The film ends with Emmanuelle dressing in front of a mirror, putting on the clothes that Mario has given her. Her reflection is just that – a reflection; a falsehood. The mirror is the blank canvas upon which Mario has created his own deviant fantasy.

Adapted from a supposedly autobiographical novel by Maryat Rollet-Andriane (although published under the pseudonym Emmanuelle Arsan), the director of *Emmanuelle* had previously worked as a fashion photographer. This background is telling: Emmanuelle's erotic scenes function more as staged tableaux than depictions of consenting adults striving for the absolute of sexual abandonment. The use of props is also evident: the film's only iconic image has its heroine, naked but for a string of pearls, reclining in a wicker chair. Elsewhere, there are billowing curtains, tempestuous rainstorms, slants of light falling through the smoky interiors of seedy clubs, cliché following cliché as if the filmmakers had worked to a checklist.

Nonetheless, it was hugely successful, generating innumerable sequels, some 'official' (Kristel headlined the first three follow-ups) and some not (the unofficial entries have the heroine's name spelled with only one 'm'). There was even the dreadful spoof *Carry On Emmanuelle* (Gerald Thomas, 1978). Not to mention the whole sub-genre of sex and style potboilers it spawned, which are still evident in many direct-to-video offerings, as well as made-for-TV fare like *The Red Shoe Diaries* and *Compromising Situations*.

Jane March and Tony Leung court controversy in *The Lover*.

There is more than a touch of *Emmanuelle* about Jean-Jacques Annaud's **The Lover** (1992), an adaptation of the novel by Marguerite Duras. Although retaining something of the melancholy musings on time and memory inherent in Duras's original, there is a similar sense of an exotic locale (Indo-china in the Twenties) as a breeding ground for sexual expression and experimentation, complete with visual metaphors (rainstorms, surging rivers) and moody, shadow-dappled cinematography.

The main characters are referred to throughout (and in the credits) only as the Young Girl (Jane March) and the Chinaman (Tony Leung). He is a businessman in his thirties, she a schoolgirl of 15½, a fact the filmmakers state twice in voice-over during the first few minutes. (The film is narrated by the heroine in old age; vocals courtesy of Jeanne Moreau.) Sent to a boarding school (cue scenes of adolescent masturbation and a vaguely lesbian tango with a fellow pupil), she meets the Chinaman and quickly becomes his lover.

It is during their first scene of intercourse that the voice-over lapses from first person past tense, to third person present, lending the proceedings an immediacy and a sense of erotic abandonment: 'He tore the dress off, he tore the little white cotton underpants off, and he carried her like that, naked, to the bed ... Fear overcomes him. He says it's not true, that she's too little ... So she is the one who does it ... She undresses him ... She touches the softness of his sex, of his skin.'

What the voice-over narrates, the camera lingers on. (It is worth noting, however, that although the Girl is shown full frontal, the Chinaman's genitals are always covered.) A scene already freighted with controversial elements – one of the participants is underage; the sex is cross-racial – is made more so by the explicit detail in which it plays out.

Naturally, it was scenes such as this that the press latched onto, the film opening to a bout of controversy, which assisted its box office performance, but nonetheless misrepresented it. *The Lover* certainly has more in its favour than most of the sex-for-its-own sake product that flourished from the mid-Eighties onwards, films whose cinema releases were often merely prologue to their shelf-life (or rather top-shelf-life) on video. Zalman King's ouevre is a case in point: *Two Moon Junction* (1989) and *Wild Orchid* (1989) both stumbled onto the big screen – the former disappearing without trace, the latter generating several column inches of 'did they or didn't they?' speculation in the tabloids over its closing scene of prolonged gymnastics between Mickey Rourke and Carré Otis (who were then an item) – before finding their true market on home video.

Of this type of film, perhaps the best known, and arguably the most successful as a cinema release, is **9½ *Weeks*** (Adrian Lyne, 1985), co-written and co-produced, unsurprisingly, by Zalman King. The plot is as negligible as *Emmanuelle*'s. Art-gallery owner Elizabeth (Kim Basinger) meets enigmatic stranger John (Mickey Rourke), and they spend the rest of the film locked in a sadomasochistic relationship. Their sexual experimentations run the gamut of masturbation, exhibitionism, striptease routines, cross-dressing, threesomes and bondage. John strives to be in control at all times, using blindfolds, whips and the application of ice-cubes to her nipples.

The most memorable scene (parodied to hilarious effect in Jerry Zucker's 1991 comedy *Hot Shots*) has John and Elizabeth introduce a culinary element when they begin having sex in the kitchen (the orthodox opportunities of the bedroom having by now presumably been exhausted). John avails himself of the contents of her fridge, applying all manner of foodstuff to her naked body, which he then consumes, a novel serving suggestion that never makes the labels of supermarket products.

If *9½ Weeks* can be said to make a point, it's that relationships engendered on a purely sexual level have no future. Particularly when said acts of intercourse become a literal battle of the sexes, issues of dominance and submission proving no stand-in for intimacy and emotionalism. The surprisingly melancholy ending sees Elizabeth, tired of John's need for control (not to mention repulsed at his white trash, penniless background), terminate the affair.

Two years later, Lyne directed another take on the casual fling gone out of control scenario. In **Fatal Attraction** (1987) the hero, Dan Gallagher (Michael Douglas), risks his marriage and professional standing (he's a successful lawyer on the verge of being made a partner in the firm he works for) over a one-night stand with emotionally insecure literary editor Alex Forrest (Glenn Close).

Their first meeting is at a book launch, where Dan is accompanied by his wife, Beth (Anne Archer). Their second, while Beth is out of town with their daughter, is when Dan is called to give a legal opinion on a possibly libellous book Alex's company is publishing. Drinks after the meeting lead from flirtation to a definite offer. Next thing, they are back at Alex's apartment, getting intimate in the kitchen (shades of Bob Rafelson's 1981 remake of *The Postman Always Rings Twice*). Dan hoists Alex onto the worktop, exposing her thighs. Her hand flails out, catching the cold-water tap over the sink. She scoops a handful and dampens her blouse with it, molding the fabric to the shape of her breast. The erotic potential – the frisson of the implicit – is quickly dissipated when she tears her blouse open, at which Dan carries her into the bedroom and the filmmakers, despite their evident fixation on the female figure, coyly cut to a scene of Dan taking his leave the following morning.

Their next, and final, sexual encounter (the rest of the film details Alex's harassment of Dan and his family when, having been dumped by him, she claims she is pregnant with his child) occurs in the elevator which takes them up to her apartment after a visit to a sleazy dance club. 'Ever had sex in an elevator?' Alex asks. 'Bet you haven't.'

Dan immediately demonstrates that, previous inexperience in this department notwithstanding, he is perfectly willing to try. Again, the film caters to the male aesthetic: Alex's legs and breasts are revealed, while Dan remains clothed. Alex stops the elevator between floors while she administers fellatio. The feet of passersby cross in front of the elevator doors, visible to Dan even as he gasps in ecstasy. Sex in dark, dangerous or semi-public places was the mainstay of *9½ Weeks*. Lyne revisits it here, whilst setting up the misogynistic ethos – sanctifying his male protagonist as a victim in spite of his philandering, egocentricity (Dan expects Beth to remain with him after he confesses to the affair) and callous behaviour (when Alex tells him she is pregnant, he blithely tells her not to worry, he'll pay for the abortion) – that informs his later foray into sexual rivalry, *Indecent Proposal* (1993).

Fatal Attraction's box-office performance indicates that it struck a major chord with moviegoers, perhaps owing to *schadenfreude* (the terrorized male is, after all, a lawyer), a misguided interpretation of the finale (Dan fails to kill Alex by drowning her; Beth finishes the job with a handgun) as female empowerment, or a collective catharsis for audience members who engaged in their own peccadillos and got away with it. Certainly, its popularity overlooks its misogyny (Dan deserves all the harassment he suffers) as well as its disingenuous closing images which focus on the sanctity of the family unit (assuming Alex's claim of pregnancy is genuine and not a ploy, when she dies, so does Dan's unborn child).

Still, a few years on, the female as villain/sexual predator is prevalent in an equally slick (and questionable) mainstream thriller. **Basic Instinct** (Paul Verhoeven, 1992) again stars Michael Douglas, this time as world-weary cop Nick Curran, who is assigned to investigate a series of murders; in each case, the victim was male and despatched during intercourse. ('Looks like he got off before he got offed' as Curran succinctly puts it at the scene of the first crime.) Curran's enquiries lead him to successful writer Catherine Tramell

(Sharon Stone), on whose novels the killings seem to be modelled. Tramell is a sensualist and free spirit, who tries out sexual partners as casually as designer outfits. Her appetites span both sexes. Against his better judgement, Curran finds himself drawn to her.

What little interest the film holds (by and large, it is a flashy, unsubtle thriller whose 'twist' can be easily second-guessed) is in seeing the unreservedly macho Curran interact with a woman who proves his equal in terms of sexual predation. In an early scene, Curran, known to his superiors as volatile and unorthodox, is compelled to attend a counselling session with Dr Beth Gardiner (Jeanne Tripplehorn). Later, he turns up at her apartment and it becomes clear they have a relationship that goes beyond the profession. Curran's sexual technique is one of self-gratification, with no thought for Beth: he pins her against a wall, tears her clothes, and finally takes her from behind, despite her protestations, in an act which can only be viewed as rape.

His treatment at Catherine's hands is pure role-reversal. She flaunts her sexuality (indeed, her bi-sexuality) at every opportunity, taunting him. She engages in a little lipstick lesbianism at a nightclub to both affront and arouse him. In their eventual act of consummation – which is more like a showdown than a love scene – Catherine uses bondage to subdue him then assumes a dominant sexual position. But even earlier than this – in the film's most memorable scene – Catherine exerts sexual control over Curran in front of his fellow detectives and Assistant District Attorney Corelli (Wayne Knight). The only woman in a roomful of men (apart from the rugged Curran, they're a sorry bunch of middle-aged,

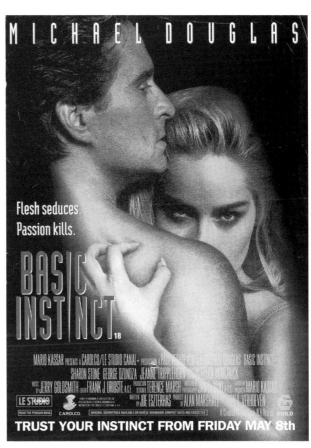

Less-than-subtle advertising for *Basic Instinct*.

overweight lechers), she nonetheless turns the incident to her advantage from the outset.

> **Corelli:** Would you tell us about the nature of your relationship [with the murder victim]?
> **Catherine:** I had sex with him for about a year and a half. I liked having sex with him. He wasn't afraid of experimenting ...
> **Corelli:** Did you ever use drugs with [him]?
> **Catherine**: Sure.
> **Corelli:** What kind of drugs?
> **Catherine:** Cocaine. [She looks at Curran.] Have you ever fucked on cocaine, Nick? [She uncrosses her legs, revealing a glimpse of pubic hair.] It's nice.

Though unsophisticated (the film's aesthetic is summed up in its title), it's an iconic moment. Nonetheless, the irony remains that for all of Verhoeven and scriptwriter Joe Eszterhas's pretensions to the empowerment of their *femme fatale*, they ultimately pander – as do most practitioners of the mainstream 'erotic thriller' – to the sensibilities of a male audience.

Homoeroticism

As we have seen with *Pandora's Box*, there is a long-standing tradition in cinema of incorporating homoerotic imagery. This generally occurs in films aimed at a predominantly heterosexual audience, to add a little frisson; and given that such films are made by men and appeal to a largely male audience, it is perhaps inevitable that these homoerotic elements tend towards lesbianism. One thinks of any number of soft-core opuses, from top-shelf direct-to-video releases such as *Animal Instincts* (A Gregory Hippolyte, 1992), to the aforementioned *Basic Instinct*. Similar titles, similar mindset: heterosexual imagery from the outset, brief flirtation with lesbianism, swift reinstatement of heterosexuality.

There are exceptions, however. ***Bound*** (Larry and Andy Wachowski, 1996) is a taut, stylishly directed film noir wherein the Sapphic relationship is crucial to the narrative. The partners in question (not to mention in crime) are Corky (Gina Gershon), an ex-con working a dead-end janitorial job at an apartment block owned by the Mob, and Violet (Jennifer Tilly), a bisexual gangster's moll. An instant mutual attraction occurs, and they not only conduct a passionate affair under the nose of Violet's short-tempered boyfriend Caesar (Joe Pantoliano), but also plot to divest him of a $2 million dollar payoff he is collecting on behalf of his boss, then leave him to take the fall.

Their efforts to carry out this scheme account for the dramatic tension of the film's second half. What makes it more effective – and raises *Bound* above any number of formulaic crime flicks rife with suitcases full of cash and treacherous double-crosses – is that the emotional vulnerability inherent in Corky and Violet's newly established relationship acts as a counterpoint to their physical vulnerability when their plan backfires and they are threatened by Caesar and his Mob cohorts, armed men for whom violence is a way of life.

The Wachowskis, who went on to make the equally stylish box office hit *The Matrix* (1999), direct *Bound*'s key moment of erotic consummation with the same degree of intensity as any of its other, more genre-based scenes. It begins as they sit in Corky's pick-up truck outside the apartment block; they have already shared two scenes of heavy flirtation, the second of which almost develops, but for Caesar's untimely appearance. Violet addresses the issue:

> **Violet:** I wanted to apologise.
> **Corky:** Oh, please. Don't apologise. If there's one thing I can't stand it's women who apologise for wanting sex.
> **Violet:** I'm not apologising for wanting to. I'm apologising for what I didn't do. [She leans across and kisses Corky.] Do you have a bed somewhere?

There is a seamless pan up from the truck windscreen, along the dark wall of some anonymous building, and into Corky's room. Dimly lit and furnished minimally, it nonetheless meets Violet's requirements. There is no further dialogue or foreplay; Corky and Violet are already intensely involved in their lovemaking as the camera emerges into their room. There follows another single, fluid camera movement, a slow circular pan around the bed. The effect is explicit and intimate, but manages to avoid being exploitative. There is a candour to the nudity which, rather than fixating on either participant's physical attributes, actually emphasizes the interconnectedness of their bodies, thus adding further meaning to the film's title.

Bound, then, distinguishes itself by showing two characters together. A similar achievement marks a turning point in **Mulholland Drive** (David Lynch, 2001). A dark satire on Hollywood and the pursuit of fame, it opens with Betty (Naomi Watts), a blonde wide-eyed innocent, arriving in LA determined to make it as an actress. The first person she meets is mysterious brunette Rita (Laura Elena Harding), who is afflicted with amnesia following a car accident. She has no idea who she is ('Rita' is a name she appropriates from a poster for *Gilda*), or what the circumstances surrounding the accident were. Betty takes pity, allowing Rita to sleep on the couch at her apartment. Friendship develops between them as they try to piece together the mystery surrounding Rita's identity.

The more they investigate, the murkier things become (they are menaced by strange characters; a body is discovered), and Rita believes her life in danger. She decides to disguise her appearance using a blonde wig[4]. The result leaves her looking not dissimilar to Betty.

> **Betty:** You don't have to wear that in the house.
> **Rita:** I was just looking at myself. I'll take it off in a minute.
> **Betty:** And you don't have to sleep on the couch either. [Rita looks unsure.] Really. Climb in bed and get a good night's sleep.

Rita removes both the wig and the towel she is clad in and complies. She kisses Betty on the cheek; a kiss of friendship. Then on the lips; a kiss of passion. Initially surprised, Betty slowly begins to respond. Neither is quite sure of herself, or of the suddenness of this unspoken revelation, and the scene is infused with an appropriate sense of hesitance. As in *Bound*, neither character is objectified (again, the scene is about their togetherness); however, there is none of the urgency of Corky and Violet's love scene. Whereas the Wachowskis' heroines are sure of their sexuality and absolute in their need for each other, Lynch depicts his in the first stages of sexual self-discovery.

Wild Side (Donald Cammell, 1996; director's cut 1999)[5] stages a pivotal scene around a similar aesthetic, as well as sharing *Bound*'s central concept of two capable, intelligent women turning the tables on the thuggish (male) criminal whose biggest mistake is to underestimate them. Alex (Anne Heche), a financial consultant forced to moonlight as a high-class hooker because of spiralling debts, finds herself catering to the brutish requirements of Bruno (Christopher Walken). A way out presents itself when she meets Virginia (Joan Chen), Bruno's ex-wife, who approaches her at the finance company. Professional relations soon become a thing of the past as Alex finds herself attracted to Virginia. A working lunch ends with them repairing to Virginia's hotel room, where Alex surprises herself by making the first move. Taking Virginia's face gently between her hands, she kisses her full on the lips.

> **Alex:** I'm sorry. I don't know why I did that … No, I do know why I did it, but I think you did it too. You're passive–aggressive.
> **Virginia** [amused]: What?
> **Alex:** You're an enigma. You're just … beautiful. And your lips are so soft. I've never kissed such soft lips before. I've never done that before.
> **Virginia:** Such innocence.
> **Alex** [concerned]: Do you like me?
> **Virginia:** I love you.
> **Alex:** Can I touch you?
> **Virginia:** Yes.

Alex slowly and tentatively places a hand beneath the jacket of Virginia's business suit, touching her skin, cupping her breast. She sinks down onto her knees as if to administer cunnilingus. Virginia reaches down, running her hand through Alex's hair, then beckons her to rise. They embrace and their lips meet. The scene that follows, while both protracted and explicit, is never exploitative. Cammell films their lovemaking naturalistically. No soft-focus, no candles, no flickering log fires, just the white expanse of daylight outside the hotel room window. Nor does the length of the scene owe to a checklist of increasingly contortionist sexual positions à la *Emmanuelle* and its imitators; on the contrary, Cammell captures the emotional complexity of Alex's sexual re-awakening as she participates in what is equally an act of love and of discovery.

For all its erotic intensity, *Wild Side* is a model of restraint (as are *Bound* and *Mulholland Drive*) compared to the first mainstream film to openly depict lesbianism: Robert Aldrich's **The Killing of Sister George** (1968). The title refers to the killing off of a soap-opera character played by ageing and curmudgeonly actress June Buckridge (Beryl Reid) when her popularity wanes with viewers and her drunken behaviour becomes intolerable to her bosses. With little in her life apart from the show (the few friends she has call her by her character's name, not her own), she takes her frustrations out on her live-in lover, Alice McNaught (Susannah York), whose life she obsessively tries to control. Alice is much younger than June, a fact that is emphasized by her girlishness: she collects dolls, flounces around like a sullen adolescent, and alternates between acting coyly and flaunting her sexuality. It's little surprise that June's nickname for her is 'Childie'.

When the decision to axe June is handed down by executive Mercy Croft (Coral Browne), Alice sees June's nemesis as her benefactor. At the 'retirement' party, while June makes a drunken spectacle of herself, Alice seeks solace from Mercy, complaining of the indignities she has suffered at June's hands. Mercy insists on escorting her back to June's apartment and helping her pack; the understanding is that Alice will then move in with her.

While collecting her belongings, Alice is sidetracked by which of her collection of dolls to take with her. As she lies on her bed amongst them, Mercy blatantly takes advantage of her, loosening her blouse and exposing her breasts, which she kisses and caresses. The camera remains on Alice's face, her eyes closing in a flutter, as Mercy's head disappears from the frame, implying a progression to oral sex. It is in this decidedly compromised position that June discovers them. Enraged, she launches into a bitter tirade that drives Alice to hysterics. Mercy tries to calm her.

> **Mercy:** Can't you see you're torturing the poor child?
> **June:** The 'poor child' wants us to pretend that she's a baby. Have a look at her ... The 'poor child' you've got there is a woman. She's thirty-two ... She had an illegitimate child at fifteen. She's got an abandoned daughter who's almost old enough to be of interest to you, Mercy dear.

Aldrich and Frank Marcus (from whose stage play the film was adapted) present a twisted view of sexual relationships, where control and gratification are the defining factors and the notion of love is notable only by its absence. That lesbianism was chosen as the microcosm for such musings makes it all the more cynical.

If *The Killing of Sister George*, never mind that it was a first in terms of the mainstream, represents something of a nadir, it hardly needs saying that lesbian cinema's most passionate moment owes to a female director: Donna Deitch. ***Desert Hearts*** (1985) is a gem of a movie, understated, beautifully played and searingly erotic. Set in the Fifties, *Desert Hearts* is a variation on the boy-meets-girl love story that has been a staple of cinema for as long as the art form has endured. Here, it's a case of girl-goes-to-Reno-to-divorce-boy, girl-meets-girl, girl-discovers-true-sexuality.

Vivian (Helen Shaver) is the divorcee, disaffected by marriage and men. Required by law to maintain a period of residency in Nevada while the divorce procedures are pending, she books in at a guest ranch run by Frances (Audra Lindley), most of whose clients are similarly divesting themselves of husbands. Here she meets Cay (Patricia Charbonneau). A sense of connection is evident between them from the outset, but when Vivian realizes that Cay is a lesbian, she worries that she might have sent out the wrong signals, and begins to keep her distance.

Much of the film plays out as an extended seduction, Cay determined to get her woman. Eventually, her persistence is rewarded as Vivian overcomes her sense of denial and admits that she is attracted to Cay. The motel-room consummation that follows is easily one of the most sensual scenes ever committed to celluloid. The set-up is simple: two women, one bed, no encumberment of dialogue but a searing tactile eroticism. Preceding *Wild Side* by a decade, it effects the same achievement: love, desire and discovery are portrayed in explicit terms, but without recourse to crudeness or cliché. This owes to Deitch's background as a director of documentaries; even within the confines of a fictive narrative, she strives for realism, for the emotional truth of her characters.

Although a film in which two sets of heterosexual relationships are played out in parallel, ***Women in Love*** (Ken Russell, 1969) was notorious for incorporating homoeroticism into a mainstream production. Adapted by Larry Kramer from D H Lawrence's novel, the narrative focuses on the friendship of Rupert Birkin (Alan Bates) and Gerald Crich (Oliver Reed), contrasting it with the relationship between the two sisters, Ursula (Jennie Linden) and Gudrun Brangwen (Glenda Jackson), with whom they become involved.

Russell's direction, attuned to Lawrence's descriptions of the liberating power of physical love, resulted in several scenes which caused controversy on the film's initial release: Rupert and Ursula running naked through a wheatfield, the camera turning through 90 degrees so that they seem to float; and a shocking cut from Rupert and Ursula lying in each other's arms after making love, to an image of the bodies of a young couple at the bottom of a lake (drained during a search for them) locked in a similar embrace.

But the pivotal – and arguably the most explicit – scene is between Rupert and Gerald. It develops from a conversation about loneliness and boredom, wherein Gerald discusses his need for physical release. He suggests the two of them box ('in a friendly sort of way, of course'). Rupert nixes the idea, but mentions that he 'used to do some Japanese-style wrestling'. They divest themselves of their evening wear, lock the door, throw a rug in front of Gerald's ornamental fireplace, coruscations of orange light patterning their naked bodies, and get to it. There follows three minutes of full frontal male nudity, close physical contact, free of dialogue except for grunts and sighs; a scene of violence between friends, violence laden with sexual tension. A sense of arousal is evident (Russell recalls that 'one of the contestants cheated by giving nature a helping hand before every take'[6]). When the bout ends, Rupert yielding to Gerald's greater strength, Russell's camera frames the moment as if it were the conclusion of a particularly heavy-handed seduction.

Notwithstanding Gerald's supremacy, he becomes decidedly uncomfortable with the situation when, lying side by side, almost touching, they talk afterward.

> **Gerald:** Was it too much for you?
> **Rupert:** No. One ought to strive, wrestle and be physically close. It makes one sane.
> **Gerald:** Do you think so?
> **Rupert:** Yes, I do. Do you?
> **Gerald:** Yes.
> **Rupert:** We are mentally and spiritually close, therefore we should be physically close, too. It's more complete. You

know how the German knights used to swear blood-brotherhood? … That's what we ought to do … We ought to swear to love each other, you and I. Intimately, perfectly. Shall we swear to each other one day?

Gerald: We'll wait till I understand it better.

While *Women in Love* dares to homoeroticize the relationship between its two male leads, the usual approach in mainstream cinema is to present homosexuality as a threat to the protagonist's sense of his own preferences. Take **Cruising** (William Friedkin, 1980) for example. An ambitious young police officer, Steve Burns (Al Pacino), accepts an assignment to go undercover in the hunt for a killer preying on New York's gay community. The milieu: leather bars and S&M clubs. Burns kits himself out with some tight jeans and T-shirts and a leather jacket, pumps a little iron, and seeks expert advice on how to send out certain signals ('light blue hankie in your left back pocket means you want a blow job, right pocket means you give one; green left side says you're a hustler, right side you're a buyer; yellow one left side means you give golden showers, right you receive').

Despite a disclaimer at the outset that the film is not representative of the gay community, *Cruising* soon settles into thematic monotony: the dynamic of every scene is the inherent threat to Burns – his masculinity, his heterosexuality, his self-identity. And yet the film resolutely avoids onscreen homosexual activity, a curious decision since the audience is thus spared the self-questioning demanded of the protagonist.

Only once does Burns come close to participating in a sexual act with another man, when he allows himself to be picked up by Skip (Jay Acovone), notorious on the scene as violent and unpredictable – chief suspect by dint of his reputation. Burns suggests a nearby motel. At this point, the film breaks with his perspective and suddenly sidelines the audience, the entire scene playing out from the point of view of the back-up team parked outside (the room already bugged). They make out just one line of conversation, Skip asking Burns if he wants to be tied up, before the signal is lost to static. A decision is taken to go in, even if it means compromising Burns's cover.

They find Burns face down on the bed, naked and hog-tied, Skip standing over him. He loses no time in assuring them (and by extension the audience) that they were in time; nothing has happened. Thus the real test of both Burns's professional capabilities and personal preferences is never addressed, nor are the audience confronted with any true insight into his sexuality.

Diametrically opposed to *Cruising's* paranoia over non-heterosexual practices, **My Beautiful Laundrette** (Stephen Frears, 1985) had audiences rooting for a couple whose relationship is not only gay but cross-racial. Omar (Gordon Warnecke) begins the film torn between the opposing world views of the two patriarchal figures central to his life: his father (Roshan Seth), a former journalist whose sensitivity to social inequity has driven him to the bottle; and his uncle Nasser (Saeed Jeffrey), the Don Corleone of the South London Asian community, whose string of businesses are a front for all manner of illicit dealings. Nasser is the free enterprise ethos of the Thatcher era personified.

Reluctantly, Omar allows himself to be palmed off onto Nasser, who starts him out in his car dealership. When the lad's financial capabilities prove more impressive than his car-washing technique, Nasser offers him something else: management of a run-down laundrette that is leaking money as surely as its machines are leaking water. After a chance encounter, Omar offers his old school-friend Johnny (Daniel Day-Lewis) a hand in the business. Johnny, reappraising his life after realizing that the National Front crowd he has been hanging around with are no more than bullies and losers, accepts. Together, he and Omar renovate the place, participating in a few of Nasser's less-than-legal schemes in order to fund the acquisition of new machines and a gaudy neon sign – POWDERS – above the premises. They also grow increasingly closer to each other, and a homosexual relationship develops, something they are obliged to keep hidden as much from Nasser – who expects Omar to marry his daughter Tania (Rita Wolf) – as from Johnny's erstwhile (still very fascist) friends.

All of the film's themes – race, sexuality, prejudice, self-identity and capitalism – achieve synthesis at the grand reopening. With a decent-sized crowd forming outside (including the NF brigade, looking for a chance to cause trouble), and Omar unwilling to open up until his father arrives, he and Johnny repair to the manager's office. Johnny starts behaving flirtatiously, but Omar is in a contemplative mood.

Johnny: Do you want to open this place up?
Omar: Not till Papa comes.
Johnny: Your father?

Omar: He went out of his way with you, and with all my
other friends, remember?

Johnny: Omar, what you on about, man?

Omar: About how years later he saw the same boys …
marching through Lewisham. It was bricks and bottles and
Union Jacks. It was 'immigrants out' and 'kill us'. People we
knew. And it was you.

Omar continues, bitterly, discoursing on the failures and
disappointments of his father's life. Johnny, unable to ameliorate the
wrong choice he made back then, can only prove to Omar the
understanding of the self he has come to be now. He embraces Omar,
then draws his jacket off and slides his hand beneath Omar's shirt. 'I
wish there was something I could do to make it up to you,' he says.
They kiss, and for a few moments, the prejudices of the past (as well,
as becomes apparent later when Johnny is attacked by the NF thugs,
as those of the present) are entirely sublimated to an act of passion.

Notwithstanding that proceedings are interrupted by the arrival of
Nasser, who blithely lets himself in, almost discovering them, it
remains a courageous scene, definitely indicative of a sea change in
the attitudes of mainstream filmmakers and audiences.

Arguably, the man who did more than anyone else to preserve artistic
integrity in gay cinema whilst retaining an uncompromising approach
to his depiction of sexual expression was Derek Jarman. A student of
art, his own work was widely exhibited in the Sixties (he won the
prestigious Peter Stuyvesant Award in 1967). He also turned his hand
to costume and set design, both in opera and film. His most celebrated
achievement in this area was his breathtaking sets for Ken Russell's
controversial 1971 film *The Devils* (see chapter five).

He made his debut with **Sebastiane** (1976), co-directed with
Paul Humfress. Loosely inspired by the martyrdom of Saint Sebastian,
often portrayed in Renaissance art as a naked young man riddled
with arrows, the film broke new ground for several reasons. Perhaps
the most striking factor is that the dialogue is entirely in Latin (much
of it, however, translates into contemporary colloquy). Not that this
was the cause of the controversy which greeted the film on its release.
Jarman's naturalistic depiction of homosexuality was unprecedented
in British cinema, his frankness underlined by a scene that showed, for
the first time in a film passed by the BBFC, an erect penis.

A darkly erotic martyrdom in Derek Jarman's *Sebastiane*.

When Sebastiane (Leonardo Treviglio), captain of the Praetorian guards at the appointment of the Emperor Diocletian (the film is set at the time of the Roman Empire), falls from favour, he is stripped of his rank and exiled to a remote garrison under the command of sexually frustrated centurion Severus (Barney James), whose disciplinary excesses are gleefully carried out by his sadistic second-in-command Maximus (Neil Kennedy). Severus becomes consumed by obsessive love for Sebastiane, but as a Christian Sebastiane refuses to engage in acts of sodomy. He does, however, find himself attracted to Maximus, but suppresses his feelings, even going so far as to mock the centurion: 'Do you think your drunken lust can compare to the love of God?'

Severus's desperation is exacerbated by the openly flaunted affair between two of his men, Anthony (Janusz Romanov) and Adrian (Ken Hicks), whose couplings he spies on. It is in these scenes that Jarman stages and photographs homoeroticism with a directness that hitherto had only been seen in heterosexual love scenes. No less effective is the pathos he brings to Sebastiane's martyrdom at the end of the film, executed by arrows, the entire garrison participating in the act.

For all that tabloid condemnation of the film fixated on the aforementioned inclusion of the image of an erection, what really makes the film contentious – and these issues are thorny, whatever one's sexual preference – is the manner in which it interlinks sex and power, desire and repression, and the self-destructive impulse towards punishment – and finally death – which drives its protagonist.

Naturally, Jarman was never going to develop into a mainstream filmmaker. Accordingly, his productions would always struggle to make it to the screen on the slenderest of budgets. Paradoxically, this seemed almost to liberate him as an artist. *Sebastiane's* Latin dialogue could never have existed in a commercial film; likewise, the mature aesthetic achievement of **Caravaggio** (1986) is rooted in the budgetary restrictions it transcends. Filmed (out of necessity) entirely in interiors, Jarman's composition and use of light invokes the very canvases of the eponymous 16th-century painter (Nigel Terry) whose life and obsessive relationship with his model and muse Ranuccio (Sean Bean) is depicted.

Caravaggio first meets Ranuccio at a boxing match, where Ranuccio's physical contact with his opponent melds the balletic qualities of filmic violence with an unabashed sense of homoeroticism, particularly at the conclusion of the bout when Ranuccio gently caresses him before delivering the *coup de grâce*. Ranuccio is quickly established as bisexual, engaged in a relationship with the androgynous Lena (Tilda Swinton), who Caravaggio also uses – as a model for Mary Magdalene.

Persuading Ranuccio to pose for him, Caravaggio pays him one gold coin per hour. Each coin the painter tosses him, Ranuccio places in his mouth to avoid breaking from his pose. At the completion of the portrait, Caravaggio places the final coin between his own lips, compelling Ranuccio into an affectation of kissing him in order to claim his payment. This is the film's most potent moment of sexual tension. Indeed, there is little actual onscreen sexual congress in Caravaggio. Jarman instead conjures a powerful aesthetic of homoeroticism from the staged tableaux, which serve as his recreations of the artist's work.

Fascinatingly, he also imbues the film with a number of contemporary references, both in terms of dialogue ('rent boy', 'piss artist', 'talent scout') and visual non-sequiturs: characters wear pristine white tuxedos, someone uses a typewriter, members of church and state dine together and divide the bill on a pocket calculator. Most tellingly, Ranuccio is seen repairing a motorbike, setting up the modern comparison of a 'leather boy'. The effect is to take what could have been an inaccessible costume drama and make it contemporary.

One of contemporary cinema's most oblique statements on homoeroticism is Neil Jordan's **The Crying Game** (1992) – by turns, a political thriller and a story of obsessive love. The opening sequence has Jody (Forrest Whittaker), a British soldier stationed in Ireland, picked up at a fairground by Jude (Miranda Richardson). He soon discovers that Jude is an IRA member. Her colleagues, led by the fanatical Maguire (Adrian Dunbar), take him hostage. The government is given three days to release a political prisoner, or Jody will be shot. The demands are not met.

Jaye Davidson as the sexually provocative Dil in Neil Jordan's *The Crying Game*.

Execution duty is given to Fergus (Stephen Rea) who, after three nights conversing with Jody during guard duty, has established a rapport – indeed, a strange sort of kinship – with him. Jody's last request before he dies (ironically, not at Fergus's hands but under the wheels of a British armoured vehicle as he tries to escape) is to pass a message to his girlfriend Dil (Jaye Davidson) in London.

Fergus, mortified as much by Jody's demise as by the reprisals (all except Maguire and Jude are killed by a British division), adopts a new identity and travels to London. He takes a job on a building site and makes contact with Dil, who works in a hairdressing salon and sings at a nearby club. Since Jody's death, she has become involved with temperamental Essex man Dave (Ralph Brown), whom Fergus loses no time in sorting out.

Fergus and Dil tentatively become involved, only for Fergus to make a discovery he is quite unprepared for. As he begins to make love to Dil at her flat, she excuses herself. Returning moments later, having changed from her little black number into a robe, Fergus reaches up and slides the garment from her shoulders, kneeling before her as he removes it. The camera pans slowly down Dil's lithe body. Moment of revelation: Dil is in possession of the full set of male genitalia. She is a he. The lush orchestral score – all lilting strings – stops dead. Fergus recoils.

On first viewing, *The Crying Game* pulls the rug from under the audience, delivering its twist as memorably as *The Usual Suspects* (Bryan Singer, 1995) or *The Sixth Sense* (M Night Shyamalan, 1999). Subsequent viewings reveal not only how easily Jordan establishes the deception (simply by having Jody refer to Dil from the outset as 'she'), but a number of little pointers that indicate things are not as they seem: Jody, Jude and Dil all have unisex names; Jody calls Fergus 'handsome' on a couple of occasions; when Fergus visits the club to hear Dil sing, the barman (Jim Broadbent) says warningly 'listen, there's something I should tell you', before being interrupted and leaving Fergus to find out for himself in memorable fashion.

Ultimately, though, *The Crying Game* transcends politics and gender; it becomes a film about acceptance. True, Fergus never experiences any doubts over his sexual identity the way Gerald does after the wrestling match in *Women in Love,* or fears that his heterosexuality is being threatened like Burns in *Cruising*, but nonetheless a relationship – indeed a sense of affection – develops between him and Dil. Fergus proves where his loyalties lie in a conclusion that veers back into thriller territory. When the vengeful Jude makes an attempt on his life, only to be shot by Dil, Fergus covers up for him and takes the fall, even though it costs him a prison sentence.

Rites of passage

If the movies considered above are concerned with their characters' sexual self-identities – either the discovery (*Desert Hearts*) or the assertion (*Sebastiane*) thereof – then an equally notable sub-genre of cinema exists which treats the formative experiences constituting its protagonists' sexual awakenings.

Perhaps the most common scenario (certainly in mainstream cinema) is the young man initiated into sexual activity by an older woman. This is a fairly comprehensive one-line synopsis of **The Graduate** (Mike Nichols, 1967), wherein Ben Braddock (Dustin Hoffman) returns to the cloying atmosphere of his family home having graduated from college, only to find that his high grades and all the career opportunities available mean nothing to him. His malaise is broken by friend of the family Mrs Robinson (Anne Bancroft). At a party hosted by Ben's parents – where, much against his will, they flaunt his academic achievements in an embarrassing show of one-upmanship – Mrs Robinson tires of the whole spectacle and asks Ben to drive her home. He obliges. She asks him in.

After a conversation fraught with implications, during which Ben becomes ever increasingly hot under the collar, Mrs Robinson takes things to a new level. Having shown Ben a portrait of her daughter, Elaine (Katharine Ross) – 'she's a very attractive girl,' Ben mumbles neutrally, looking at her portrait – Mrs Robinson begins to disrobe in front of him, insisting he help her with her zipper. Ben makes his excuses and flees downstairs. Mrs Robinson asks him to bring her purse up before he leaves ('just put it in Elaine's room'). When he concurs, she appears behind him, her naked form reflected in the glass of Elaine's picture as she closes the door and blocks his exit.

Here's to you, Mrs Robinson: the younger man and the older woman in *The Graduate*.

Ben: Oh God. Let me out.
Mrs Robinson: Don't be nervous.
Ben: Oh God, get away from that door.
Mrs Robinson: I want to say something first.
Ben: Jesus Christ.
Mrs Robinson: Benjamin, I want you to know that I'm available to you and that if you won't sleep with me this time –
Ben: Oh my Christ!
Mrs Robinson: – and if you won't sleep with me this time, I want you to know that you can call me up any time you want and we can make some kind of an arrangement. Do you understand what I'm saying?
Ben: Yes, yes. Let me out.

The editing during this exchange is as subliminally brilliant as that of the shower scene in Hitchcock's *Psycho*; at each of Ben's interjections there is a brief jump cut (lasting no more than a single frame) to a close-up of Mrs Robinson's naked body. The juxtapositions with Ben's expressions – which range from shock to arousal to abject self-consciousness – are as hilarious for the audience as the situation is disconcerting for Ben. Nonetheless, it is not long before he enters into an affair with her, no matter the potential for social embarrassment and disenfranchisement (Mrs Robinson's husband is Ben's father's business partner), and the destructive effect it threatens with regard to his considerably more socially acceptable relationship with Elaine.

A similar situation, albeit one that plays out in an economically depressed small town in Texas in the Fifties (a time and place that couldn't be further removed from the moneyed suburban milieu of *The Graduate*), occurs in **The Last Picture Show** (Peter Bogdanovich, 1971). Here, Sonny Crawford (Timothy Bottoms) and his best friend Duane Jackson (Jeff Bridges) while away their high-school years shooting pool and trying to go all the way with their respective girlfriends. When Sonny breaks up with Charlene (Sharon Taggart) after she refuses to proceed beyond first base, he finds himself responding to the frail beauty and emotional vulnerability of Ruth Popper (Cloris Leachman), wife of his baseball coach.

Their love scene, at which he finally loses his virginity, is conducted in silence, emphasizing how awkward both parties find it. There are moments of potential embarrassment: Sonny catches his knee on the bedside table as he hops around taking his shoes off; Ruth gets entangled in her slip as she tries to remove it. Neither say a word to each other. They finish undressing beneath the sheets, removing their underwear. Sonny adopts the missionary position, getting down to business with nothing in the way of foreplay. Bogdanovich refrains from soundtrack music; their coupling is conducted to the ungainly creaking of the bedsprings.

Sonny and Ruth's affair plays out in counterpoint to the equally undignified experiences Duane's on–off girlfriend Jacy (Cybill Shepherd) puts herself through. Concerned that Duane is not good enough for her, she whores herself to the country-club set from the other side of town. Attending a midnight swimming party, she undergoes the ritual of disrobing in plain view of everyone on the diving board, only to be rejected by a potential rich-kid boyfriend for being a virgin. Later, she invites the advances of an older man, a business partner of her father's, and ends up all but raped on a pool table for her troubles.

The Last Picture Show is a film that tells several stories, none of which have happy endings. The stark but beautiful black-and-white cinematography is as much an elegy for a lost time as it is for its characters' compromised lives – lives which, as the film is honest enough to demonstrate, are often more blighted than ameliorated by the promise of sex and the hope of romantic fulfilment.

Equally removed from the mainstream conventions of a happy – or at least unambiguous – ending is the conclusion reached in Alfonso Cuarón's **Y Tu Mamá También** (2001), which presents another take on the older-woman scenario. This time, however, her presence increases an already extant sexual rivalry between two friends, Julio Zapata (Gael García Bernal) and Tenoch Iturbide (Diego Luna). Nor does she provide their first sexual experience – both have girlfriends with whom they are sexually active – but acts as the catalyst for something else. Julio and Tenoch meet Lusia Cortés (Maribel Verdú) – like Mrs Robinson, a family friend – while they are killing time: school is over and their girlfriends have decided to go backpacking around Europe. Initially, they are content to attend parties and get high.

Soon, though, they become bored by their lot in life. A chance meeting with Luisa provides the impetus they need. The estranged wife of a pompous novelist friend of the Iturbides, she seeks out the boys' companionship after she leaves her husband. They regale her with stories of an idyllic beach they are planning to spend their summer at, a fictitious place to which they give the name 'Heaven's Mouth'. To their delight and surprise, she offers to accompany them. Their odyssey develops on two levels: (a) avoidance of destination and (b) mutual attraction to Luisa's womanly charms. En route, she entices both of them. While equally enthusiastic, neither proves capable of any degree of finesse. Their technique borders on the premature. Moreover, each grows absurdly jealous at the other's dalliance with Luisa.

The real reason behind their fractiousness comes to light only at the very end. By chance, they discover a beach that boasts all the qualities of the fictitious Heaven's Mouth. A drunken evening at a beach bar, where Luisa dances provocatively, ends in some three-way action back at their hotel room. Initially, the scene focuses on Luisa.

The camera dwells on her physical looks, particularly once the element of nudity is introduced. However, her presence is soon dispensed with. Having helped the boys out of the clothes, she goes down on them, sinking out of the frame entirely. Until this point, she has filled the space between Julio and Tenoch – as she has done throughout the entire journey. Now, however, they are naked, sexually excited and closer to each other than at any time before. Tentatively at first, then with more feeling than they ever demonstrated with their respective girlfriends, the homoerotic tension between them is finally resolved.

A poignant and downbeat coda has them meeting in a coffee shop a year later, their friendship discontinued. Conversation is awkward. Both have split up with their girlfriends and drifted into indifferent relationships with other women. They are still, essentially, in denial of their true sexuality. This is what differentiates *Y Tu Mamá También* from many films of its ilk. Instead of being just a vulgar sex comedy – one can imagine, had the production been American, it would have been made in the style of, say, *Porky's* (Bob Clark, 1981) or *American Pie* (Chris and Paul Weitz, 1999) – it emerges as an honest study of emotional confusion and the bonds and boundaries of friendship.

So far we have considered films that explore the rites of passage theme from a predominantly male point of view. The 'older woman' figure is in the foreground, and the protagonists' responses have been defined by either nervous agitation or raging hormones. A much different perspective is gained, however, when the central character is female.

Bernardo Bertolucci's **Stealing Beauty** (1996), set amongst the rural splendour of Tuscany, is a paean to sexual awakening. Following the death of her mother, Lucy Harmon (Liv Tyler), a 19-year-old American, visits the home of expatriate family friends Ian (Donal McCann) and Diana Grayson (Sinead Cusack).

On a previous trip there, as a younger teenager, she had a brief holiday romance with Niccolo (Roberto Zibetti), a friend of the Graysons' son Christopher (Joseph Fiennes). It is her intention to rekindle the flame; to lose her virginity to him. Niccolo, however, is a changed man; he flaunts his success with other girls, and doesn't hide the fact that his interest in her is just sexual – nothing more. When he attempts to seduce her amidst the stony ground of an olive grove, his behaviour proves emotionless, his whispered platitudes ('Lucy, I'm dying for you') blatantly insincere. Accordingly, she rejects him.

Later, she finds solace in the companionship of Osvaldo (Ignazio Oliva), a young shepherd. Under a hazy late-afternoon sky, they sit looking out across open fields. As Lucy reminisces about her mother, she starts to cry. Osvaldo puts a consoling arm around her, his eyes filling with tears as well.

> **Lucy:** Why are you crying?
> **Osvaldo:** Because I want to kiss you and I'm not able ... I can't.

Slowly, she leans into him and kisses him. Very tenderly, he reciprocates. Bertolucci cuts to another scene, returning to them as night falls. They have begun to make love. A campfire burns nearby, bathing their skin in a warm orange hue. For the amount of flesh on display, full nudity is never effected. The scene is gentle and slowly paced; erotic, not explicit. The emphasis is on the consensual: even as Osvaldo is ready to enter her, he asks, 'Can you help me, please?'

Poles apart from the grubby couplings of *Last Tango in Paris*, Bertolucci portrays his young heroine's loss of virginity as unimpeded by awkwardness or discomfort, an act of love as lyrical and pastoral as the landscape in which it is set.

Catherine Breillat's *À Ma Soeur* (2001), on the other hand, considers the issues of control and coercion in adolescent sexual experience. A savage subversion of one of the staples of teenage fiction – the holiday romance – the basic scenario has sisters Elena (Roxane Mesquida) and Anais (Anais Reboux) holidaying with their mother on the French coast, only for an already fraught atmosphere to erupt into hostility when the underage Elena loses her virginity to Fernando (Libero de Rienzo), an Italian student.

Elena is 15 years old, has inherited her mother's glamorous looks and, for all that she flaunts her developing sexuality, is naive and easily swayed. Anais, 12, overweight and eternally consigned to the background, is cynical and world-weary. Elena believes in love and wants her first time to be a romantic occasion, an act of giving to somebody who cares about her. Anais sees it as simply an act, something to be done without love just to bring an end to the stigma of being a virgin.

By the end of the film – with Elena duped by Fernando, the family attacked as they return home and Anais sexually assaulted – Breillat forces us to compare, and ask ourselves how different, essentially, are the two explicit scenes the film centres around: Fernando's protracted, psychologically manipulative persuasion of Elena to yield to him; and the swift, brutal rape of Anais by a complete stranger.

Predictably, it was this final scene that generated controversy (although passed uncut on its cinema release, *À Ma Soeur* was cut by almost a minute and a half for home video/DVD). Disturbing as the rape scene is, the 20-minute sequence detailing Elena's seduction by Fernando is an equally uncomfortable viewing experience. Questions of intimacy and betrayal of trust are raised from the outset, as Elena entertains Fernando in her bedroom – the room she shares with Anais, whom she instructs to keep her eyes averted (thus equally heightening and compromising her sister's emotions). Her come-on to Fernando (she dresses in a provocatively flimsy nightgown, allows him into her bed and instigates foreplay) soon develops into a situation she has no control over. 'Swear you won't do it,' she pleads, quickly realizing that she does not want to go all the way. Fernando has none of it, hands all over her, sweet nothings whispered distractingly in her ear. By means of cajolery, emotional blackmail and blatantly insincere promises of love, he eventually persuades her into anal sex ('all the girls take it the back way'). Not only does he subject her to the degradation of sodomy, but also has the temerity to suggest that it doesn't even count as sexual intercourse.

Ultimately, Elena and Anais suffer equally ignominious fates at the hands of men motivated by a need to misuse women. The only difference is that Elena's betrayer is a good-looking smooth-talker … and that her ordeal lasts considerably longer.

Just as shocking in its visceral content as *À Ma Soeur*, Larry Clark's **Kids** (1995) offers what could be described as a remorselessly depressing view of mankind – except that its morally challenged anti-heroes aren't even men. The title is accurate: all of Clark's characters are in their mid-teens. Sex is not the longed-for and desperately pursued holy grail the teenagers of *The Last Picture Show* regard it as; it is something as taken for granted as broken families, cheap booze and easily scored drugs. This is the environment that has spawned Telly (Leo Fitzpatrick) and Casper (Justin Pierce), foul-mouthed losers who steal what they cannot be bothered to earn, whose only aim in life is to have sex. Preferably – as far as Telly is concerned – sex with virgins. 'No diseases … no skank, just pure pleasure,' he muses as the film opens. Not, it transpires, that this aesthetic of hygiene applies to Telly himself.

The narrative – or what passes for it (*Kids* has a loose, semi-improvised feel) – follows Telly and Casper through a single day as they roam the urban wasteland of New York (a grim but effective metaphor for the emotionless wasteland that is their lives). Contrapuntally, Jennie (Chloe Sevigny), one of Telly's earlier conquests, scours the city looking for him, wanting to confront him with the results of her AIDS test; with the knowledge that he has made her HIV-positive.

By the time their paths intersect, it is nightfall. Telly has taken his latest victim, Darcy (Yakira Peguero), to a party at Casper's house (the latter's parents are conveniently out of town). Jennie is barely conscious by the time she arrives, having become progressively drunk throughout the day. Her intent is to prevent him from infecting anyone else. She fails. He is already having intercourse with Darcy when Jennie stumbles in on them. 'Shut the fucking door,' he exhorts, not even glancing up from his ministrations.

Too drunk to do anything else, she finds a couch to fall asleep on and immediately loses consciousness. The day has one final ignominy for her. Casper, irked that he hasn't got laid, never mind that he's hosting the party, finds himself sitting next to her. Realizing that she's going to offer no resistance, he progresses from feeling her up, to removing her jeans and underwear and raping her.

'I like fucking,' is how Telly justifies himself as the film ends, and there can be no doubt that, with the transference of disease between Jennie and Casper, he has 'fucked' his best friend in one sense of the word just as surely as he has 'fucked' Jennie, Darcy and any number of young girls in both senses.

More in keeping with the lyricism of *Stealing Beauty* is the perspective offered in Nicolas Roeg's **Walkabout** (1970). Pre-credits, a paragraph of explanatory prose defines the title: 'In Australia, when an Aborigine man-child is sixteen, he is sent out into the land. For months he must live from it ... Eat of its fruit and flesh. Stay alive ... The Aborigines call it the WALKABOUT. This is the story of a "WALKABOUT".'

This said, the film opens in a city (the very image of modernity) and quickly identifies its protagonist as female. Thus a polarity is established: traditionalism/contemporaneity; masculinity/femininity.

The cityscape is soon left behind for the vastly different terrain of the outback, captured with a sense of timelessness[7]; a place of beauty and of danger. This sense of removal from the everyday world, this stripping away of conventional trappings, is enhanced by the film's refusal to identify any of its characters by name. With the exception of a few peripheral characters, the majority of the running time is occupied by just three people: a 14-year-old girl, her younger, prepubescent brother, and an indigenous youth of 16, undergoing the 'walkabout'[8].

A shocking betrayal of innocence by the adult world sets the narrative in motion. The Girl (Jenny Agutter) and Boy (Lucien John) are driven into the outback by their father (John Meillon), ostensibly for a picnic. The Girl smooths out a blanket and organizes the food while her brother plays on a nearby rock. Suddenly their father, whose behaviour has been tense and insular, begins shooting at them with a pistol. The Girl carries her brother out of harm's way and they shelter in a culvert. Their father douses the car in petrol and a final shot rings out. When they emerge, he is dead and their only means of transport is wreathed in flames.

Still clad in their school uniforms, they begin a long walk through the outback, without map, compass or supplies. Their odyssey takes on a different perspective when they meet the Aborigine (David Gumpilil). Slightly older than the Girl, who initially regards him suspiciously, he strikes up an instant rapport with the Boy, never mind that they do not share a common language.

Thus far, the film's emphasis on sexuality has been confirmed to the Girl, particularly the dubious erotic connotations of her school uniform. Now a half-naked, older (but still adolescent) male is introduced into the equation. The Girl, despite her attempts to cling on to a 'civilized' mode of behaviour (at one point she berates her brother for neglecting his dress and appearance: 'we don't want people thinking we're a couple of tramps'), fixates on his near-nudity. Later, when the Aborigine encourages the Boy to climb a tree, the Girl joins in, at first struggling to keep her skirt from riding up and revealing her underwear, but quickly losing all sense of self-consciousness.

The developing relationship between the trio (they increasingly come to resemble an ersatz family) contrasts with an almost comedic vignette at a weather station, where the staff comprises five men and a woman. The woman is blonde, athletic and dressed in a white blouse and short skirt – a more womanly equivalent of the Girl's school uniform. Whereas the Girl and her companions by now represent the wilderness, the meteorologists stand for the scientific/ rational/'civilized' world. And the comparison couldn't be more effective. The men at the station break off playing cards (they use a deck depicting topless women) in order to ogle their female colleague's legs and breasts, craning their necks like schoolboys in order to achieve a better view. Roeg then cuts to a scene – all the more sensual for its air of innocence – of the Girl, having finally abandoned the social conventions she has been holding on to, swimming nude in a pellucid and unpolluted lagoon.

An apposite moment, here, to mention *Walkabout* as a precursor of the likes of *The Blue Lagoon* (Randal Kleiser, 1980), where the nubile charms of a girl on the cusp of womanhood (Brooke Shields in Kleiser's film) provides the big tease which the filmmakers never quite deliver on. The difference, of course, is that *The Blue Lagoon* and its ilk are no more than soft-focus outings, which, while not actually fitting the description of pornography, are tailored to the same voyeuristic part of the psyche.

For all that Roeg depicts full-frontal nudity, *Walkabout's* bathing scene is neither prurient nor gratuitous. It is the culmination of his development of the untamed landscape and the feral intensity of the natural world as a metaphor for a young girl's sexual awakening – something that is all the more pure and emotional for being distanced from the cynical and image-conscious modern world.

Emphasizing the extreme: the cinema of Nicolas Roeg

Walkabout is perhaps Roeg's most accessible – certainly his most linear – film. It was preceded by **Performance** (1970), which he co-directed with Donald Cammell. *Performance* is so non-linear, so multi-layered that even its title works on at least four levels. The opening sequence intercuts a Rolls-Royce gracefully purring along a country lane with footage of Chas (James Fox) having violent sex with his girlfriend Dana (Ann Sidney), slapping her and holding a horsewhip across her throat. So already 'performance' refers to the car (symbolic of the materialistic lifestyle of Chas and his gangster associates), as well as sexual performance. Chas, an enforcer for gang boss Harry Flowers (Johnny Shannon), is known in underworld parlance as a 'performer', hence a third meaning.

The entry into the film of reclusive rock star Turner (Mick Jagger) suggests another meaning: the singer's performance, i.e. his adoption of a stage/public persona that masks his true self. A ringmaster in a circus of shifting sexual identities, Turner plays out his fantasies in the arms of his two willing groupies, the voluptuous Pherber (Anita Pallenberg) and the androgynous Lucy (Michele Breton). ('You're very skinny,' Chas tells Lucy at one point, 'like a little boy or something.') An early scene of a threesome between Turner, Pherber and Lucy is filmed and edited so ambiguously that one is never quite sure whose body is whose.

Chas and Turner's worlds collide when Chas goes on the run after Flowers has him beaten for getting out of line. (He is also sexually humiliated, stripped and his buttocks whipped.) Chas fetches up at Turner's decaying townhouse and a psychosexual power game ensues. Needing to alter his looks for a passport photograph (Chas has made provision to obtain false papers and thereby leave the country), he allows Turner and Pherber to remodel his image. They get him high and dress him up in clothes that parody his gangster image, then in a wig and robe that render him half effeminate, half Christ-like. Later, when Pherber seduces him, she holds a mirror to his chest so that her breast is reflected, and then over his face so that hers is superimposed. Chas does not like the implications.

Sexual power games: Edward Fox is caught between Anita Pallenberg and Mick Jagger in *Performance*.

Pherber: Do you never have a female feel?

Chas: No, never. I feel like a man. A man. All the time.

Pherber: That's awful. That's what's wrong with you … It's a man's man's world.

Chas: There's nothing wrong with me. I'm normal.

Pherber (laughing): How do you think Turner feels like? … He's a man, a male and female man.

Chas tries to silence her by forcing himself on her, but she continues to taunt him. A pan away from the bed reveals Turner watching them. Pherber tells Chas that Turner sees in him the potency and aggression that he has lost as a musician. Stoned, Chas confronts Turner in his studio. A shared hallucination sees Turner assume Chas's identity (as well as delivering a blistering rendition of 'Memo from Turner'); the moment is rife with homoeroticism as Turner proves more effectual in controlling his colleagues than Chas ever was, compelling Flowers and his heavies to strip in front of him. This not only visualizes the shifting of sexual identity from Chas to Turner, but also revisits the homoerotic tensions of the male-dominated gangster milieu as evidenced in the earlier scene of sexual humiliation against Chas.

If *Walkabout* marks a transition from the claustrophic interiors of *Performance* to the sweeping grandeur of the outback, then Roeg's next film **Don't Look Now** (1973) combines elements of the two, internalizing its characters' relationships while clearly establishing a sense of place. The difference is in the types of sex Roeg is representing: the extreme sexual experimentation of *Performance*, enacted for the sake of nothing more than self-gratification (and arguably portrayed for the purpose of being in a position, as director, to push the boundaries), is utterly at odds with the more 'normal' representation of sex in *Don't Look Now*, where the act serves to re-establish emotional connections between man and wife, a theme that is not just conventional, but almost biblical, tying in with the film's religious overtones.

Traumatized by the death of their daughter, who drowns in a pond near the family home, John Baxter (Donald Sutherland) and his wife Laura (Julie Christie) relocate to Venice where they try to regain some meaning in their lives. John becomes involved with the restoration of a church; the mosaic on which he works is a perfect metaphor for

Roeg's typically fractured approach to narrative. So too is the church's disrepair redolent of Venice as a whole. A dank city of narrow waterways and buildings whose dilapidation belies their former glories, it is reminiscent of Luchino Visconti's wonderfully melancholy *Death in Venice*, made just two years earlier.

While John immerses himself in his architectural endeavours, Laura meets two sisters, one blind and claiming to have the gift of second sight. Laura's belief in the possibility of beyond-the-grave communication with her daughter not only lends the film its supernatural undertones (a precognitive vision John has, which he mistakes for an incident grounded in the present, unwittingly leads him to his death at the film's sinister denouement), but tests her relationship with her husband, who cannot bring himself to give credence to such stuff. The tragedy is that, just before this additional strain is placed on a marriage already tested to its limits, John and Laura achieve, if not full emotional reconciliation, then certainly a re-attainment of intimacy. What Neil Sinyard describes as 'the most passionate love scene in British film'[9] begins almost clinically as they perform their ablutions before turning in. The nudity is very naturalistic; the lighting not necessarily flattering. Perhaps the only deliberately eroticized image is when John turns to look at Laura and sees her posed, naked, in front of a mirror. The caught glimpse; the reflected image – the moment is almost voyeuristic.

The scene shifts – appropriately – to their bedroom. In direct contrast to the usual male-orientated sex scene in which the man is clothed or semi-clothed while nudity is required of the woman, Roeg has John lounging on the bed, reading an article, completedly naked; Laura, however, is demurely clad in pyjamas. She reaches out to touch him – a symbolic act, since this is the first time they have been intimate since the loss of their child – and their tactile communication succeeds where their verbal communication has failed. Roeg intercuts their lovemaking with scenes of them dressing prior to going out to a restaurant, which reminds us that, as a married couple, sexual intercourse is as much a part of the fabric of their lives as social intercourse.

It is worth noting that their coupling is quite inelegant, not only making the scene seem more real – actual sex as opposed to the flatteringly shot and physically perfect cinematic variety – but hinting at the desperation inherent in their need for each other. Perhaps uniquely, this is cinema not just showing an act of union, but of reunion. But Roeg still has one more element to bring to the scene: when they speak to each other during the act, the dialogue is not recorded (there is only the soundtrack music), thus preserving the sense of intimacy which is the emotional aesthetic of the entire scene.

Roeg's use of sexual imagery is just as central to **The Man Who Fell to Earth** (1976), but this time the emphasis is not on the human aspect of it; in fact, completely the opposite. His main character is an alien. Said being does, however, turn up on earth with the benefit of an anglicized name (Thomas Newton), a British passport (Roeg leaves this procurement unexplained[10]), and a business plan. Newton (David Bowie, whose distinctive ethereal looks have never been better employed) uses his home planet's advanced technology to found, on earth, a corporation that achieves global success. This, however, is part of

Candy Clark discovers the truth about David Bowie in *The Man Who Fell to Earth*.

what brings him down. A shadowy syndicate (possibly with criminal connections) plots his downfall, scared that his firm's technological innovations will have a negative effect on consumer trends. An associate, scientific researcher Dr Bryce (Rip Torn), betrays him, mistrustful of Newton's obsessive secrecy. On one level – and the film is a multi-layered, multi-faceted experience – *The Man Who Fell to Earth* plays out as an examination of Newton's attempt to assimilate, while ultimately being betrayed by, a myriad of human experience.

At one point, he watches a bank of television screens, perhaps two dozen of them, his eyes flicking between the vastly different images, until finally he screams, 'Get out of my head!' The media proves as debilitating to him as the world of big business. Just as problematic is the realm of human emotionalism. Newton becomes involved with a small-town girl, Mary-Lou (Candy Clark), who looks after him when he falls ill after checking in at the hotel where she works. She progresses from nurse, to personal assistant, to constant companion, and eventually to lover. Their consummation is intercut with scenes of Newton giving her a high-powered telescope as a gift. Their lovemaking is tentative, almost cautious – they caress and trace the outlines of each other's body. By alternating these moments with shots of them taking turns looking into the firmament, Roeg establishes a sense of sex as an act of exploration and discovery.

However, a different, much darker, aspect soon becomes apparent. The second time Mary-Lou has sex with Newton, it is in the full knowledge that he is an alien. She finds herself repulsed by him; their relationship disintegrates. As with so many other films – the film noirs discussed in chapter one, for example, or the horror movies considered in chapter four – sex is a harbinger of something nasty, a pleasure for which the protagonist must pay. Newton is betrayed by Bryce, kidnapped by the syndicate whose monopoly he threatens and incarcerated. He becomes a shambolic drunk. Mary-Lou is allowed to visit him, but what follows is more like a hooker and her client acting out a seedy fantasy than an emotional reunion. Newton, drunk, threatens Mary-Lou with a pistol that turns out to be a blank-firing replica. He dips the barrel in a glass of wine (a phallic object made damp by its introduction into a circular receptacle – you don't have to study Freud to work it out) and licks it. The tone is set for a scene that jettisons the tenderness and intimacy of before, and replaces it with the notion of sex as a weapon. The pistol is brandished by both of them during a frenzied and loveless session; it is discharged several times. The final montage of close-ups of the pistol's gaping barrel are intercut with shots of Newton and Mary-Lou's first sexual encounter, a succinct statement of all that has been lost.

In opting to use an alien as protagonist, the theme of outsiders so prevalent in Roeg's fims – the gangster adrift in a drug-addled netherworld; the English schoolgirl lost in the outback – is given its fullest statement. Despite the commercial success of *Performance*, *Walkabout*, *Don't Look Now* and *The Man Who Fell to Earth*, there is nothing mainstream about any of them. With his deconstructive narratives and emphasis on often extreme imagery, Roeg's work has more in common with European cinema than British or American traditions.

As we have already noted, European films generally tend to treat sex with an openness that is often missing from their mainstream counterparts. This frankness has proved a defining feature of European fare; the next chapter considers the influence of this aesthetic.

the european
aesthetic

CHAPTER THREE

We have seen the mainstream approach to onscreen sexuality in American cinema: the avoidance of the explicit and the use of metaphor (chapter one); and, latterly, sex as a commercial raison d'être in the 'erotic thriller' sub-genre (chapter two).

With the exceptions of Nicolas Roeg, whom we have just considered, and Peter Greenaway (whose work is covered later in this chapter), British cinema's attitude to the subject does not, by and large, bear thinking about. While the Sixties delivered a number of commendably gritty 'kitchen sink' dramas where the emphasis was more on the consequences of sex – usually unwanted pregnancy: see, for example, *Saturday Night and Sunday Morning* (Karel Reisz, 1960) or *Up the Junction* (Peter Collinson, 1967) – than the act itself, the Seventies saw a marked aesthetic downturn with a succession of dire sex comedies such as *Percy* (Ralph Thomas, 1971) and *No Sex Please, We're British* (Cliff Owen, 1973). Unerotic and unfunny, the nadir was reached with the *Confessions* series, starring Robin Askwith, their titles (*-of a Window-Cleaner, -of a Driving Instructor*) and content as interchangeable as any of the *Carry On* films.

The common denominator of both series is that they take the guilty, snickering aspect of seaside postcard humour to its ultimate conclusion. They represent a depressing inability of both filmmaker and audience to confront sexuality in a candid, emotionally exposed, and mature manner. The natural comparison that this creates to European cinema reveals a more frank, less embarrassed, and commendably confident approach to the representation of sex. This chapter considers the work of five groundbreaking directors, and the thematic concerns which run through their filmographies.

Luis Buñuel

Luis Buñuel began a career in cinema that was to stretch across six decades as an assistant director in Paris, where he had settled after leaving his native Spain, in 1926. Two years later, in collaboration with the groundbreaking surrealist artist Salvador Dalí, he made *Un Chien Andalou*. It was the first of many controversial works, and he followed it with the equally provocative *L'Âge d'Or* (1930), a blatantly anti-clerical work where the intrusion of the church upon the liberties of the individual is stated in the protracted metaphor of a young couple being prevented from consummating their passion.

Much of Buñuel's first two decades behind the camera was spent away from his homeland. He spent most of the Forties and Fifties in Mexico, where the absurdist qualities of his early works were replaced by the social realism of *Los Olvidados* (1950) and *Ensayo de un Crimen* (1955).

On his return to Spain he made ***Viridiana*** (1961), only to have it promptly banned. In Italy, it was denounced by the Vatican. Catholic disapproval was inevitable. Consider the basic narrative: the eponymous heroine (Silvia Piñal), a novice on the verge of taking her vows, inherits a country estate and decides to do her bit for the community, allowing a group of beggars, invalids and social pariahs to make their home there. Her reward is mockery when they hold a drunken banquet, a scene Buñuel composes in deliberate parody of da Vinci's 'The Last Supper'. Just to up the ante on the satire, their wanton, lecherous behaviour plays out to the strains of the 'Hallelujah Chorus' from Handel's *Messiah*.

Borderline necrophilia in Buñuel's *Viridiana*.

If it was this sequence, principally, that caused controversy (Buñuel was threatened with arrest and legal proceedings if he entered Italy), equally contentious was the scene which establishes Viridiana's ownership of the estate. Called away from the convent where she has been devoting herself to study and prayer, she visits her uncle, Don Jaime (Fernando Rey), whom she is under the impression is in ailing health. It turns out that he is quite well, but nursing an unhealthy obsession with her. Viridiana, it transpires, bears a considerable likeness to the Don's late wife, who died on their wedding night. He proposes to her, but she is shocked and rejects him, insisting she must return to the convent. Don Jaime asks one favour of her before she leaves, to which she reluctantly agrees: to wear his wife's wedding gown.

She is unaware that Don Jaime has already coerced his maid into drugging her coffee. When she passes out, still clad in the wedding dress, he carries her into the bedroom, arranges her hands across her chest as if she were a corpse laid in an open coffin, and bends to kiss her. He loosens her dress, exposing her breasts, against which he places his head. Then he stops, horrified by the nature of his own intentions. He leaves the room.

The next morning, in a blatant act of fabrication, he tells Viridiana he had her while she was asleep, knowing that by allowing her to believe she is no longer a virgin, she cannot go back to the convent. Again, he is mortified by his own actions; this time, he hangs himself, leaving the estate to his niece.

Viridiana is one of Buñuel's most focused films, its *mise en scène* unfolding naturalistically, not in the fragmentary, overstylized manner of, say, *The Milky Way* (1968) or *The Phantom of Liberty* (1974); its hour-and-a-half running time constitutes a sustained satire on church and state. It is ironic, then, that the scene described above, bereft of religious imagery, presents one of Buñuel's darkest statements on the human condition.

If *Viridiana* is an allegory – a dark irreligious parable, almost – then **Belle de Jour** (1967) is both an update and a role-reversal of an already controversial piece of work. The key to the film is its heroine's name: Séverine. It is a feminization of Severin, the protagonist of Leopold von Sacher-Masoch's *Venus in Furs*[1] who gains sexual satisfaction from being whipped, beaten and humiliated. The term *masochism* is derived from Sacher-Masoch's name as *sadism* is from the Marquis de Sade's.

A stylish satire on the hypocrisy and degeneracy of the middle classes, Buñuel's film also blurs the lines between reality and fantasy, and employs its moments of masochism to this end. Séverine (Catherine Deneuve) is the bored trophy wife of society doctor Pierre Serizy (Jean Sorel), for whom she feels affection but not attraction. After a year, their marriage remains unconsummated. Pierre's friend, the lecherous Henri Husson (Michel Piccoli), propositions her with tedious regularity. *Ennui* permeates her life.

For no better reason than curiosity, she takes a position at a brothel; she is given the name Belle de Jour after insisting she can only work afternoons. Clients include the owner of a chocolate factory whose endearments are as cloying as his product, but who demonstrates a distinctly unsaccharine attitude towards Séverine as soon as they are left alone together; a Chinaman with an ornamental box, the (unrevealed) contents of which repel some of the girls and fascinate others; and a gangster with gold teeth who becomes obsessed with Séverine.

Masochism as iconography: Catherine Deneuve in *Belle de Jour.*

Séverine also encounters two men who like role-play. One is a pitiful businessman who insists on being whipped for some imagined transgression while pretending his dominatrix is a noblewoman. More disturbing is the Duke who insists she dress in a winding sheet and lie in a coffin. He places asphodels on her unmoving body and delivers a eulogy during which he refers to her as his 'daughter'. It is hinted that he completes this ritual by crawling beneath the coffin and abusing himself.

But are the fantasies of these individuals any less questionable than those of Séverine herself, fantasies that lead her to the brothel in the first place? The very first scene in the film establishes Séverine's mindset.

She is driving along a country road in a landau with her husband, Pierre, when he suddenly complains about her frigidity. Ordering the horsemen to stop, he further instructs them to haul her out of the carriage. He watches as they bind her hands and tie her to a tree. He rips her blouse, exposing her back, and tells them to flog her. This done (she seems to enjoy it), he gives them leave to take their pleasure with her. The scene immediately cuts to the Serizys' bedroom, Séverine sitting demurely in bed, nightgown buttoned to her neck, refusing Pierre's attentions.

'I struggled with it for fifteen minutes': Fernando Rey denied by a chastity belt in *That Obscure Object of Desire*.

If Séverine's perceptions are oblique, her fantasies in diametric opposition to her actual sexual persona, then those of Mathieu (Fernando Rey) in ***That Obscure Object of Desire*** (1977) are skewed to the point where he sees Conchita, the dancer he becomes obsessed with, as two separate women. One of them, feral and voluptuous (played by Angela Molina) fans his ardour, while the other, aloof and unattainable (Carole Bouquet) constantly denies him.

Buñuel's usual targets are present and correct: the middle classes (Mathieu is a successful businessman who uses either bribes or his contacts in the legal profession to get his way); the church (Conchita's mother, supposedly devout and God-fearing, enters into a financial arrangement with Mathieu in return for her daughter's hand in marriage); the state (the battle of the sexes – in itself a metaphor for power and control – is played out against a backdrop of terrorist activity).

Many of these themes are personified by the train passengers – a lawyer (the state; officialdom), a psychiatrist (a comment on the nature of Mathieu's behaviour), a mother and daughter (symbolic of the family unit Mathieu can never achieve from a paid-for marriage) – to whom Mathieu narrates the story. Amusingly, the teenage daughter is sent out into the corridor as Mathieu describes his night of non-consummation.

Initially reticent following her mother's bargain with Mathieu, Conchita nonetheless agrees to live with him, and quickly begins treating him as something of a sugar daddy – an easily manipulated older man she can sponge off, while avoiding for as long as possible the necessity of intercourse with him. Their first night together sets the tone. He enters the bedroom with Conchita (Molina), who goes into the bathroom to change; she dons a nightgown, which she leaves unbuttoned, her breasts exposed. The Conchita who rejoins him (Bouquet) is demurely presented. True, she reluctantly reveals herself to him, allowing him the briefest of caresses, but then announces, 'Not yet. I'm not in the mood now.'

Mathieu expresses his frustration then forces himself upon her. She doesn't struggle, but insists he extinguish the candles. He does then returns to her. 'Don't celebrate your victory too soon,' she says as he fumbles beneath the covers. With a grunt of surprise, he leaps out of bed and relights the candles. Beneath her nightdress, Conchita is wearing what can only be described as resembling a chastity belt as if designed by Janet Reger.

'I struggled with it for fifteen minutes,' he tells his fellow passengers; 'I was incensed. There were so many knots and laces, and with Conchita struggling –' he shrugs helplessly ' – it was impossible to remove it.'

The final dark joke of *That Obscure Object of Desire* is, of course, that Mathieu never gets to have his way with her. In casting two actresses in one role, Buñuel takes to its logical extreme the concept of a woman for whom one's passion is unrequited as having two sides: the erotic and the unattainable. And in structuring an entire film around a man being denied sex with a beautiful woman (in what can be seen as a throwback to *L'Âge d'Or*), Buñuel creates one of cinema's most finely crafted metaphors for sexual frustration.

Bertrand Blier

There is more than a touch of Buñuel in the works of Blier, who takes an equal delight in challenging the sensibilities of the middle classes and toying with the notions of image and perception (the latter most notably in *Merci La Vie*, discussed later in this section). His first significant film, **Les Valseuses** (1974)[2], is, however, less a satire on the middle classes from within à la *Belle de Jour*, as a visitation upon them of two amoral louts from the wrong side of the tracks. Said louts are Jean-Claude (Gérard Depardieu, in the role that made his name) and Pierrot (Patrick Dewaere), a pair of 20-somethings for whom the concepts of honesty, gainful employment and social conformity are utterly alien. Within the first half-hour, they give chase to, sexually harass and rob of her purse an overweight middle-aged housewife; bait a security guard in a supermarket (they steal a trolley out of spite when his vigilance prevents all other attempts at shoplifting); go joyriding in a stolen car; and take hostage Marie-Ange (Miou-Miou), the wife of the car owner, when he pulls a gun on them.

Worse is to follow: the protracted sexual harassment of a young woman on a train; the cultivation of an older woman, Jeanne (Jeanne Moreau), as their own private sexual plaything; their joint deflowering of the 16-year-old Jacqueline (Isabelle Huppert), daughter of the family they terrorize and whose car they steal (each successive automobile is abandoned every time a *gendarme* appears) at the end of the film. But none of these acts is as blatantly misogynistic as their treatment of Marie-Ange, who seems to cross their path at each stage of their aimless odyssey across France. When they originally take her hostage, they prostitute her without a second thought to the garage owner they are relying on for provision of a getaway car. 'What's wrong with this chick?' he demands of them afterwards: 'She just lies there and stares at the ceiling.'

Later, encountering her again, Jean-Claude and Pierrot (who share women as freely as they share the profits of their thievery), take turns with her, determined to bring her to orgasm. The scene is framed such that Pierrot's buttocks, rising and falling, are seen in the foreground while Jean-Claude, seated behind them, looks on. While Pierrot tries, unsuccessfully, to get a reaction, Jean-Claude criticizes his technique. 'Take your time,' he urges; 'negotiate.'

Pierrot gives it up as a bad job and Jean-Claude takes over. The framing is still the same: one performs, the other watches. Jean-Claude keeps up a running commentary: 'The keynote is flexibility. Take it easy … Now rev it up, get the motor going. Then ease down, gentle again. Take your time. Make her impatient … And now shift into fourth,' for all the world as if he were discussing the handling of a Citroen. Not that any of this has the slightest effect on Marie-Ange, who lies there yawning.

The fact that the only communication during this athletic bout (athletic on Jean-Claude's part, at least; Marie-Ange might as well be asleep) is between the two friends only adds to the sense of homoeroticism already present in their scrutiny of each other's sexual practices.

Blier takes a more elegant approach in **_Trop Belle Pour Toi_** (1989), his satire on middle-class social mores. The title translates as 'too beautiful for you', a reference to the glacially perfect looks of Florence Barthelemy (Carole Bouquet), wife of successful car-dealership owner Bernard (Gérard Depardieu). On the surface, Bernard has it all: profitable business, dream house, trophy wife, two well-behaved children. But he puts everything on the line when he meets Colette Chevassu (Josiane Balasko). She arrives to fill a temporary clerical position. Engrossed in a telephone conversation, he barely glances at her as he directs her into the office. Seconds later, having dealt with his caller, Bernard wanders in to introduce himself. They shake hands. Neither makes a move to let go. A look passes between them. There is a moment of perfect silence, which speaks volumes.

Colette is everything Florence isn't: dowdy, unglamorous and slightly overweight. Bernard's friends, once news of the affair gets out, speculate endlessly as to what the attraction is. Bernard's rejection of the more beautiful woman is the key to Blier's deconstruction of middle-class values and pretences. Bernard, one of the in-crowd for as long as he has Florence on his arm, is really as much of an outsider as Colette: working class (he refers to himself as a 'mechanic'), it is his wife and his money which give him social credence.

Trop Belle Pour Toi differs from _Les Valseuses_ not only in its more restrained approach, but in the surprisingly emotional portrayal of romantic and sexual love. Colette's soliloquy to Bernard as she watches him through the glass partition which separates their offices – a declaration of love he cannot hear – is a poignant moment, understated and beautifully played. Their acts of consummation, in which Colette's dowdiness is replaced by passion and radiance, are as tender as they are erotic. A scene where Colette describes her pleasure in terms of his, the two of them naked, close together, the most gentle of caresses passing between them, is a love letter made visual.

> **Colette:** Shall I tell you what I want? … It's pleasure I want, the pleasure you'll pump into me drop by drop just by letting your veins pulse inside inside me … then I shall gently disgorge you back inside you.

91

Bernard: I love you.

Colette: You mustn't say 'I love you'. Just listen, I'm telling you what I want ... I want to make your heart burst with anticipation.

While the satire in *Les Valseuses* and *Trop Belle Pour Toi* is mainly aimed at notions of class and social conditioning, **Merci la Vie** (1991) – perhaps Blier's most Buñuel-esque project – casts its net wider. Starting as something of a role-reversal of *Les Valseuses*, it develops into a meditation on reality, fantasy, fiction, time, memory, relationships, sex and human suffering.

The startling opening image has Joëlle (Anouk Grinberg) beaten and kicked by her Porsche-driving boyfriend for nothing more than meeting him dressed in a wedding gown ('it was a joke,' she protests). Abandoned, she is befriended by sullen teenager Camille (Charlotte Gainsbourg). Together, they embark on a series of amoral misadventures – within the first quarter of an hour they have jointly seduced a stranger and stolen and written off two cars – that Jean-Claude and Pierrot would be proud of. Not that these early examples of road movie escapism are developed. The girls mostly find themselves travelling from one town to the next on foot (which makes for a slower example of the genre than even *The Straight Story!*). Besides, they soon encounter a film crew. The producer takes a shine to Joëlle and offers her a part.

From here on in, *Merci la Vie* operates on any number of levels: reality, fiction (there is a film-within-a-film, the narrative and director of which keep changing), memory and fantasy. The latter is most evident in a scene where Camille visits her parents while they are still childless and harangues her father, instructing him to impregnate her mother ('I'm impatient to be born').

If this seems to indicate some cynicism on Blier's part towards marriage (the opening scene is literally a slap in the face to that most romantic of images, a young bride dressed in white), then his take on sex itself is nothing short of abject. None of *Trop Belle Pour Toi*'s romanticism is on display. Instead, having aroused audience sympathies for Joëlle, Blier suddenly uses her as a metaphor for the spread of the HIV virus. A flashback has her deliberately infected by the sinister, if laughably named, Dr Warm (Gérard Depardieu). 'Suppose I import an illness?' he suggests to one of his colleagues, ushering Joëlle into his office. 'Tests, research ... an epidemic could be very profitable.' There follows a montage: Joëlle, her feminine charms emphasized by low-cut tops or flimsy negligées, seducing a variety of men. The sequence ends with her sharing breakfast with the less than good doctor, her hair dishevelled, her bathrobe open to her breasts. 'You've got to screw everyone capable of getting it up,' he exhorts her.

Indeed, one can read the whole film as a metaphor for AIDS. An extended sequence towards the end of *Merci la Vie* draws a parallel between the disease and the holocaust of World War II. A questionable comparison, perhaps, but Blier effectively demonstrates that every age has its horrors, and that the horror of the modern age stems from the very act that ought to ensure propagation.

Federico Fellini

Two helicopters cut through the sky above Rome. Beneath one is a statue of Christ, as imposing as the one which overlooks Rio de Janeiro. In the other is Marcello (Marcello Mastroianni), the tabloid journalist covering the transportation of the idol. Not that his mind is 100 per cent on the job. Spying a group of girls in bikinis sunbathing on a rooftop, he signals the pilot to swing back and descend for a better view.

So begins ***La Dolce Vita*** (1960), Fellini's unforgettable portrait of modern malaise. Every element of the film communicates a sense of despair. Marcello – the audience's guide – makes his living harassing celebrities and sniffing out scandal[3]. The film perforce renders everything in terms of fame, image, scandal and sex. The absence of God echoes through a succession of set pieces: a false miracle; an organist playing Bach's 'Toccata and Fugue' in an empty cathedral; a seance; a ghost-hunt.

The absence of emotionalism is just as acutely observed. 'Our parties are like first-class funerals,' one of Marcello's acquaintances muses; while another soliloquizes about 'the three great oblivions: smoking, drinking, bed.' The physical takes precedence, as embodied early in the film by American starlet Sylvia (Anita Ekberg), met at the airport by crowds of admirers. Marcello becomes smitten with her, to the chagrin of his suicidal fiancée Emma (Yvonne Furneaux). Although Sylvia's centrality to the narrative is short-lived (her burgeoning affair with Marcello is cut short by her jealous manager),

Anita Ekberg cavorts in the Trevi Fountain in *La Dolce Vita*'s most iconic and erotic image.

she represents a potent symbol of the empty hedonism that characterizes the lives of everyone in the film. Her dance routine, which precedes the famous Trevi fountain scene, is akin to Rita Hayworth's in *Gilda*: it is burlesque, a flaunting of her voluptuous sexuality, as much a denial of her availability as an exhibition of her charms.

If the subsequent sight of Sylvia cavorting in the Trevi fountain, her already revealing black dress now damply moulded to her hourglass figure, gives *La Dolce Vita* its most iconic and erotic image, a grimmer view of emotionless sexual abandonment is reserved for the finale. In a scene that pins down the moral decay of the middle classes as effectively as anything by Luis Buñuel, Marcello (having argued with Emma and scorned her declarations of affection for him) attends a party hosted by socialite Nadia (Nadia Gray). The occasion: the annulment of her marriage. Religion and love have already been dismissed; now even the sanctity of marriage is denigrated. Marcello complains that the party is going with less than a swing. Somebody suggests an exotic dance routine. The cry goes up: 'Let the hostess strip'. Nadia obliges. The lights are dimmed; an appropriately sleazy bit of rumba is played.

It promises to be an erotic highpoint, conforming to the aesthetics of self-expression in dance and musicality considered in chapter one: all narrative concerns sidelined, allowing the woman complete centrality. Not so. Fellini increasingly cuts away to Nadia's less-than-overwhelmed audience, who drift into desultory conversation as their interest wanes, exchanging snide remarks and titbits of gossip. Marcello ends up talking to somebody about his car.

The striptease ends with Nadia semi-recumbent, removing her shift from beneath her fur wrap. Marcello leans forward and removes this final item. Fellini cuts to Nadia's ex-husband withdrawing into the shadows, a handful of sarcastic remarks following him. In *Gilda* and *From Dusk Till Dawn*, the dance routines are about empowerment. Here, the emphasis is on depersonalization.

That a more celebratory view of womanhood is offered in **Guilietta degli Spiriti** (1965) – *Juliet of the Spirits* in its English-language title – is hardly surprising since the eponymous heroine is played by Fellini's wife Giulietta Masina. This represents an audacious piece of casting, given that, during the course of the film, Guilietta's husband Giorgio (Mario Pisu) conducts a none-too-discreet affair with a younger women (a fashion model to boot) and eventually leaves her, whereupon she is tormented by voices, including that of a childhood friend who committed suicide for 'romantic' reasons and who exhorts her to do the same.

The voices are the culmination of a series of visions, dreams and memories that merge with Guilietta's already compromised sense of reality. For Guilietta is a woman who has lived her life in the shadow of others: primarily her husband, an adulterer for whom she has selflessly subjugated her own passions and ambitions, and her glamorous party-girl neighbour Susy (Sandra Milo), whose colourful lifestyle redoubles Guilietta's conviction that her own is sadly lacking.

But she soon discovers that the gaiety of Susy's world is a veneer hiding emotional emptiness. Invited to a party, which she attends alone after Giorgio makes another pitiful excuse to see his mistress, Guilietta realizes that the champagne and finery are simply a prelude to functional sexual encounters. Susy's palatial house is decorated like a brothel, with ceiling mirrors and slides connecting bedroom to pool (for the easier facilitation of post-coital skinny-dipping). It is in one such bedroom that Susy leaves Guilietta, assuring her she will be joined by a young stud. Guilietta tries out the bed, considers herself in the mirror. The youth appears and lies down beside her.

The sexuality that Fellini conjures here is akin to that orchestrated by Buñuel in *That Obscure Object of Desire*: everything is prelude; there is no payoff. While Mathieu in Buñuel's film does not achieve consummation because Conchita continually denies him, in Guilietta's case it is self-denial – albeit a self-denial she is shocked into by a vision of the Virgin Mary wreathed in flames.

This re-assertion of Guilietta's Catholic sensibilities also acts as something of a corrective to *La Dolce Vita*'s opening shot, where the concept of religion is helicoptered out of the film so that nothing can intrude upon Marcello and friends' chic nihilism for the next three hours.

If *La Dolce Vita* can be seen as a carnival of hedonism and grotesquerie, albeit peopled by pretty young things, then **Fellini-Satyricon** (1969) dispenses with the veneer of designer chic and goes all out for the grotesque. The fragmented, dreamlike narrative and bizarre imagery are more in keeping with *Juliet of the Spirits*, but where that film was characterized by a sense of melancholy sensualism, *Fellini-Satyricon* takes a different and much darker approach to its characters' sexuality. The title derives from a work by Gaius Petronius, a satirical account written in the first century AD of life in Rome; Fellini's adaptation (co-written with Bernardino Zapponi) is loose in every sense of the word, and seeks not so much to present historical verisimilitude as suggest, impressionistically, the essence of the times.

The opening scenes are comparable to *Sebastiane* (see chapter two), all togas and homoeroticism, the camera lingering on the male body. Encolpius (Martin Potter) and Asciltus (Hiram Keller), sometime friends and now sexual rivals, fall out over the youthful, androgynous Giton (Max Born). When Giton chooses Asciltus, Encolpius, distraught and defeated, embarks upon a series of misadventures which variously see him coerced into a gay marriage to the captain of a slave ship, conned into a gladiatorial contest with a minotaur and mocked at every turn, Asciltus invariably showing up to steal any number of possible conquests from under his nose. The characters that populate these tenuously linked episodes are, by and large, repulsive caricatures, individuals for whom one would be hard put to muster any degree of sexual attraction. It says something that, for a film so steeped in sexuality (particularly Encolpius's guilt over his attraction to those of the same sex), acts of intercourse are minimal and generally suggested rather than depicted. Even when a coterie of attractive concubines enter the picture, they do little more than whip Encolpius across the buttocks for being disinterested in girls.

The sexual tension between Encolpius and Asciltus is brought sharply into focus in a scene where, having escaped the slave ship, they seek shelter in what they believe is an empty house. Not so. They find a slave girl hiding in one of the rooms. To their surprise, she is responsive to their presence and instigates sex. They lie side by side as she straddles them. Close-ups frame them together. Her centrality to the scene is gradually reduced. As with *Y Tu Mamá También* (see chapter two), the focus is on the unspoken attraction between the two men.

As pivotal as this moment is (everything leading up to it emphasizes Encolpius and Asciltus's sexual rivalry; for the rest of the film Encolpius experiences guilt/denial over his homosexuality), Fellini swiftly curtails it. This is in keeping with *Fellini-Satyricon's* fractured and incomplete narrative (the film ends in the middle of a sentence!), and also serves to mirror the unresolved nature of the characters' sexuality. Fellini's questioning, in *La Dolce Vita*, of the value of the sexual act when performed purely for physical gratification, is here taken to another level: sex enacted orgiastically, almost as a competition, the concepts of love and intimacy never entertained. Encolpius's denial of his attraction to Asciltus is a further indication of the depersonalization which has resulted from his emotionally deficient approach to sex.

Pedro Almodóvar

Homoeroticism is a staple of Pedro Almodóvar's early work, as are nymphomania, transsexualism and prostitution. *Pepi, Luci, Bom* (1980), *Labyrinth of Passion* (1982), *Dark Habits* (1983) and *What Have I Done to Deserve This?* (1984) are full of colour, manic plots and oddball characters (*Dark Habits* features a nun who pseudonymously writes pornographic novels) proving the order of the day.

The scatter-gun narratives of these films gave way to a darker, more intimate vision. *Matador* (1985)[4] marks something of a turning point. Sexual concerns remain in the foreground (as they do in all of Almodóvar's work), but the aesthetic becomes more character-based. The element of high camp becomes less conspicuous in his protagonists' sexual behaviour, replaced by sinister, more ambiguous motivations.

Having said that, the early scenes of **Tie Me Up! Tie Me Down!** (1989) seem to hark back a decade. Kitsch, colour and general bad taste are all present and correct as ex-porn star Marina (Victoria Abril) makes her bid for thespian legitimacy in a cheesy

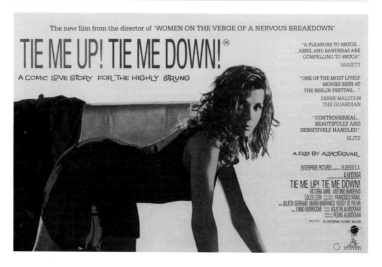

Provocative title, provocative image: poster art for Almodóvar's film.

B-movie whose wheelchair-bound director Maximo (Francisco Rabal) is obsessed with her (he abuses himself over videos of her hardcore productions, then leaves ludicrous messages of love on her answering machine). Even more questionable are the actions of Ricky (Antonio Banderas), a mental patient recently released back into the community. It is when he puts into operation his less-than-meticulously-thought-out plan to win Marina's affections that the film moves away from the madcap tone of earlier Almodóvar films *Dark Habits* or *What Have I Done to Deserve This?*.

Ricky, who once had a one-night stand with Marina (she remembers nothing of this, largely due to her significant drug habit), has thought of nothing but her during his period of institutionalization. Now, he kidnaps her. This constitutes stage one of his grand design. It is some indication of his intellectual limitations that stage two consists of nothing more sophisticated than sitting around and waiting for her to fall in love with him.

During the course of her incarceration at chez Ricky, a relationship of sorts evolves between the two. Ricky, for all that he uses the trappings of bondage to effect the tying up and tying down of the film's title, proves very gentle towards her, catering to her every need.

At first appalled by her habit, but unable to refuse her (even though bound, she quickly begins to exercise a form of dominance over him), Ricky agrees to score drugs for her. Kidnapping he may have a talent for, but the milieu into which the search for illegal substances leads him is one he is ill-prepared for, and he sustains a beating at the hands of a dealer. Freeing Marina from her bonds when she offers to treat his wounds, not only is she as good as her word, but they end up making love.

As cynical as it may seem, as unnatural a form of courtship as Ricky's actions may be, Almodóvar plays their sex scene as a celebration, a consummation, of the feelings that are now reciprocal between them. There is none of *Matador*'s sex-as-death or, as we shall see, *Live Flesh*'s sex-as-revenge ethos. When Ricky and Marina make love, it is just that: an act of love. And Almodóvar's achievement is that the scene is as tender as it is erotic.

If *Tie Me Up! Tie Me Down!* works as a twisted love story (a two-hander for most of the running time, it's basically a boy-meets-girl narrative with kidnapping and bondage thrown in), **Live Flesh** (1997) establishes a panoply of shifting relationships; an almost tesselating pattern of sexual connotations between its characters. Victor (Liberto Rabal), a young man whose mother was a prostitute, becomes obsessed with a woman from the opposite end of the social spectrum: Elena (Francesca Neri), the hedonistic, dope-smoking daughter of a diplomat. Victor loses his virginity to her in a drunken fumble in the toilets at a nightclub; a week later, he bluffs his way into her flat, intent on seeing her again. She mocks him, calling him a 'wanker' and scorning his technique. Then she pulls a gun and orders him to leave. They struggle and the gun discharges.

Called to the incident are two cops, the young and dynamic David (Javier Bardem) and the borderline psychotic Sancho (Jose Sancho), who drinks heavily and obsesses over the string of affairs his wife Clara (Angela Molina) is carrying on. Victor, panicking, holds Elena's gun to her head. David negotiates with him, persuading him to release Elena. Sancho then tackles Victor. In the struggle, David is wounded.

Fast forward six years: David is confined to a wheelchair; Elena, motivated by a newly found social conscience, has become his wife (he can pleasure her only through oral sex) and is working at a home for disadvantaged children; Victor has just left prison and entered into an affair with Clara, who is still married to the abusive Sancho. Consumed with thoughts of revenge, Victor begins stalking Elena, even managing to secure himself a position as a volunteer at the home (this despite his criminal record!). When Victor learns from Clara that the fateful incident was orchestrated by Sancho as a revenge on David, who was amongst her lovers, things take a different turn. He confesses his intent to Elena: that he sought to seduce her, pleasuring her in ways that David cannot, thereby revenging himself. Later, Elena visits him at his digs; disrobing before him, she tells him that afterwards he must never see her again.

Almodóvar films the subsequent scene with such attention to the form and shape of their naked bodies (one shot has them embracing so tightly that there is some ambiguity as to whose body is whose) that they seem to be disconnected from their surroundings, as if they were having sex weightlessly. The effect is striking; from the darkest of motives, Almodóvar creates a love scene that is transcendental. As with the film noirs considered in chapter one, however, it is also a prologue to further acts of violence. And since all the sexual relationships in the film were instigated by moments of violence, Almodóvar's dark, erotic vision gains a perfect symmetry.

Talk to Her (2002) marks a return to the self-contained, character-based narrative of *Tie Me Up!, Tie Me Down!*, boasting four lead roles, two of whom are comatose throughout most of the running time. Again, Almodóvar explores the excesses of a twisted love story. There are two 'couples' involved: Benigno (Javier Cámara) and Alicia (Leonor Watling), and Marco (Dario Grandinetti) and Lydia (Rosario Flores). Alicia and Lydia are both hospitalized, the former following a car accident, the latter (a female bullfighter) after being gored. Both are in comas. Marco, a journalist who began a relationship with Lydia after interviewing her for an article, keeps vigil at her bedside. This is how he comes to meet Benigno. Friendship develops between them.

Marco is representative of normal behaviour: grief-stricken, very much in love with Lydia (who, crucially, has reciprocated his advances), he has every right to be there. Benigno's motives, though, are as questionable as Ricky's in *Tie Me Up!, Tie Me Down!*. His medical training, his acquisition of professional qualifications and his position at the hospital have all been gained with the sole purpose of bringing him closer to Alicia. Benigno's obsession with Alicia, a classically trained dancer, begins as voyeurism with him watching her at practice from his adjacent apartment (which he shares with his mother). He takes to stalking her, going so far as to gain access to her apartment and prowl around her bedroom. Indeed, it is because of Benigno's clumsy overtures, and her subsequent flight from him, that her accident occurs.

As socially unacceptable as Benigno's behaviour has been thus far, a small sliver of humanity is engendered within him through his friendship with Marco. However, when Marco disappears from the scene (having discovered that Lydia was on the verge of leaving him and returning to her ex-boyfriend), Benigno's unhealthy attentions towards Alicia are redoubled. He crosses the line in disturbing fashion, having intercourse with her while she is still comatose. Since this is an act of non-consensual sex, Benigno essentially rapes her, leaving her pregnant. The ensuing physiological changes result in her re-awakening.

Almodóvar poses a similarly thorny moral condundrum to that of Dennis Potter's groundbreaking television drama *Brimstone and Treacle* (in which a young girl, mute, regains the power of speech as a result of sexual trauma): that out of an undeniably reprehensible event, something occurs that can be considered positive. Dangerous ground, but Almodóvar's sympathies are never in the wrong place: Benigno pays for his crime - incarcerated, he commits suicide while awaiting trial.

Almodóvar's fearlessness in confronting his subject matter is matched by his directorial genius in the visual metaphor he uses to reflect the psychosexual drama being played out at the hospital. Alone, without Marco's companionship, Benigno kills time one evening by attending a screening of a silent film, *The Shrinking Lover*. In a brilliant pastiche of the rubbery effects and cheesy acting of many a Fifties B-movie, a scientist accidentally shrinks himself. He is rescued by his girlfriend, whom he agonizes about being unable to fulfil sexually; moreover, even lying next to her in bed proves a threat when she almost squashes him turning in her sleep. Finally, he is able to overcome both problems only by climbing inside her vagina.

This bizarre and provocative sequence, for all that the vaginal effects are obviously phony (as evidenced by the film's 15 certificate!), challenges the audience with an explicit but surreal metaphor for an implicit but horribly perverse reality.

Peter Greenaway

It would be easy to call Peter Greenaway a surrealist – there is an artifice, a theatricality, to much of his work, not to mention a preponderance of visual non-sequiturs – but to do so would overlook the importance he places on structure and formalism. Which is not to say that he is in any way beholden to narrative or convention (an early film, *The Draughtsman's Contract* [1982], succeeds in being a murder mystery without a solution).

The only literal thing about **_Drowning by Numbers_** (1987) is the title: there are four deaths by water, and the whole film is suffused with numerology. The opening scene has a young girl skipping as she calls out the names of a hundred stars. The numbers one to a hundred are incorporated into the fabric of the film, be they painted on cows, tagged to dead fish, hung on boards as cricket scores, or displayed as identifying marks on runners' shirts or swimmers' caps. Greenaway structures the narrative so that a tale of conspiracy, murder and cover-up is interspersed with a series of games, ranging from hangman's cricket to tug-of-war.

Amidst this tapestry of mathematics and metaphors lurks the equation, quintessential to Greenaway's work, of sex and death. The murder element of the story revolves around three generations of women – grandmother, mother, daughter (Joan Plowright, Juliet Stevenson and Joely Richardson respectively) – all named Cissie Colpitts, who respond to the burden of unsatisfactory husbands by doing away with them. Helpfully referred to in the credits as Cissie 1, Cissie 2 and Cissie 3 (the three Fates? the three Furies?) – by descending order of age – Cissie 1 sets the tone by holding her husband Jake (Bryan Pringle) down in the bath after she catches him fooling around with a half-witted village girl.

Pandering to the libido of middle-aged widower and local coroner Henry Madgett (Bernard Hill), she not only promises him sexual favours if he issues a 'natural causes' death certificate, but intimates that her (younger) relatives will also be so inclined. By the time he realizes she is holding out on him, his services are called on again. Cissie 2, bored with her sexless marriage to businessman Hardy (Trevor Cooper), has taken advantage of his ill-advised après-meal swim and made sure he goes under. Against his better judgment, and still in hope of carnal gratification, the coroner does their bidding.

By the time Cissie 3 has seen off Bellamy (David Morrissey), her husband of three weeks (the number three again), suspicions have been aroused and pressure is being put on Madgett to reveal the truth. But the women hold sway over him, and the coldly logical finale sees him literally in too deep. As in _That Obscure Object of Desire_, the withholding of sex provides the darkly comic payoff. Before leaving him to sink (swimming isn't an option: he can't), they suggest he might want to disrobe, thereby making his death look more like an accident. 'Alone in an open boat with the women you love and an invitation to undress,' as Cissie 3 teasingly puts it.

The denouement takes on an ironic hue given its prefigurement in the orchestration of Bellamy's death in a scene where the sex/death/water themes find their most explicit synthesis. Like Madgett, Bellamy is a non-swimmer. Cissie 3, who harbours ambitions of swimming to Olympic standard, offers to teach him. In a deserted swimming pool, she soothes his frustrations at his aquatic inabilities by instigating sexual proceedings, peeling off her bathing suit and diving underwater to remove his trunks. What follows is less *The Last Picture Show* than Bellamy's last rites: she also removes his floats and distances herself from his thrashings with an elegant backstroke, then treads water for a while as she waits for him to finish drowning.

As the symmetry and symbolism of *Drowning by Numbers* indicates, the interconnectedness of things is a constant theme in Greenaway's films. In **The Cook, the Thief, His Wife and Her Lover** (1989), the title again proves literal, sketching out the dynamics of the eternal triangle (the cook acts as the lovers' willing accomplice) at the heart of the film's narrative. The cook is Richard Borst (Richard Bohringer), gastronomic maestro at the upmarket restaurant where boorish London crime boss Albert Spica (Michael Gambon), the thief, holds court. Albert's wife Georgina (Helen Mirren), despite her fear of his frequently demonstrated capacity for violence, enters into an affair with Michael (Alan Howard), a quiet and unassuming bookshop owner who is also a regular at the restaurant. Michael is the antithesis of the verbose, profane Albert. Nonetheless, they are connected as much by their relationships with Georgina as by their choice of restaurant. The centrality of the restaurant (until the film relocates to Michael's apartment in the last half-hour, every scene takes place there) is emphasized in Richard's complicity in Michael and Georgina's affair, allowing them the run of his establishment for their liaisons.

Greenaway also establishes connections between gastronomy and cannibalism, sex and death, eating and bodily functions ('the naughty bits and the dirty bits are so close together,' Albert pontificates, 'that it just goes to show how eating and sex are related'). It is apposite, then, that Michael and Georgina's first sexual encounter occurs in the ladies' toilets. A case of *coitus interruptus* as it turns out, Albert blundering in demanding to know what's keeping her.

Further couplings occur in storerooms and the meat store, the latter providing a juxtaposition of human flesh and animal flesh that prefigures Michael and Georgina's escape from the restaurant after their affair has been discovered: still naked from lovemaking, they are hustled into the back of a lorry hauling meat, sides of beef and – grotesquely – the head of a cow swaying with the motion of the vehicle.

There is a low-key eroticism to their encounters, but mostly these interludes provide moments of quietness and tenderness amidst Albert's extended bouts of physical violence (doled out as freely to his own men as to his enemies) and histrionic verbiage. Naturally, once Albert is informed of his wife's infidelity, his rage is boundless. He tracks Michael down and has him killed, suffocated as page upon page torn from his collection of books are crumpled and forced down his throat.

Georgina's revenge, in the graphic finale, brings together all of the film's themes. Arranging a surprise dinner for Albert, the main course cooked by Richard to her specifications, she lays on a welcoming party of Albert's victims, the abused and beaten, the insulted and vengeful. Outnumbered and disarmed, he is forced to sit at a table laid for one. The meal: Michael's corpse, cooked, garnished, served with all the trimmings. 'Try the cock,' Georgina instructs him at gunpoint, 'it's a delicacy. And you know where it's been.' This takes to an extreme the food/sex correlation suggested in *Tom Jones* (see chapter one) and revisited in soft-core terms in *9½ Weeks* (see chapter two). Unique outside of, perhaps, Marco Ferreri's *La Grande Bouffe* (see chapter five), Greenaway extends the equation to food/sex/death.

By complete contrast, **The Pillow Book** (1996) fashions poignant connections between art, sex and self-expression, in the combination of calligraphy and the naked human body, so that words of intimacy take on the erotic quality of their own definition.

The memory of a face-painting ritual when she was a young girl (the words a birthday greeting from her father) remains with Nagiko (Vivian Wu) into womanhood. Named in tribute to Sei Shonagon, the 10th-century diarist from whose classic work the film takes its title, Nagiko is encouraged by her parents to keep a diary. As her sexuality develops, she equates the smell of paper with the scent of a lover's skin. Soon, the inscription of characters, sentences, whole sections of prose onto her body by her lovers becomes a necessary part of sex.

Until she meets Jerome (Ewan McGregor), an English translator living and working in Japan, this body-calligraphy remains a one-way process. She soon complains that good lovers are invariably bad

Sexuality in terms of cleansing and purification in Greenaway's *The Pillow Book*.

calligraphers and vice versa. Jerome, however, offers her his skin: 'Use my body as the pages of a book – your book.' This invitation can be seen as an extension of the intimacies of a diary – a suggestion Greenaway illustrates the first time Nagiko and Jerome make love: using split screen, he simultaneously shows her writing up the encounter in her journal afterwards. She is propped up in the bath while she pens this bit of prose. This proves a pertinent image, since the words have to be washed from the body before the lovers can reclothe themselves. It is an image Greenaway revisits when Nagiko and Jerome have sex in an overflowing bath.

In this respect, calligraphy as a form of sexual expression proves more intimate than a diary, since the words are washed away; therefore, the content of what has been written is only ever retained in the memories of the lovers.

pleasure and payment

If the rites-of-passage films examined in chapter two are concerned with adolescent sexual awakening, then a very different take on the subject is offered by Krzysztof Kieslowski's ***A Short Film About Love*** (1988). Like its similarly-titled predecessor *A Short Film About Killing* (1988), it began life as an episode of *Dekalog*, a series of hour-long films (originally produced for Polish television) based on the Ten Commandments, which Kieslowski then expanded to feature length for a theatrical release.

A Short Film About Love centres on 19-year-old Tomek (Olaf Lubaszenko), a postal clerk. Excruciatingly shy and socially incompetent, his only friend (with whose mother he lodges) is serving overseas with a UN peacekeeping force. His lifestyle is solitary; his sole interest is in Magda (Grazyna Szapolowska), an older woman, free-spirited and promiscuous, who lives in the adjacent apartment block. He spies on her through a telescope he keeps trained at her window. He sets his alarm clock for the hour she arrives home. He dials her number then hangs up wordlessly when she answers (though he does call back, in a poignantly gauche moment, to apologize). He takes a second job delivering milk to the flats in the morning so he can get closer to her. Eventually, he compromises himself professionally, sending out bogus notifications of money transfers to lure her to his place of work.

This ploy backfires quite spectacularly, and Magda is accused of fraudulent behaviour by post-office officials. Tomek, appalled, confesses to her. She responds by entering into a sexual power game with him. She seduces her lover in front of the window, knowing Tomek is watching, then tells the fellow he is being watched. (He gives Tomek a not-so-friendly warning in the form of a blow to the face.) Finally, she brings Tomek back to her flat. Wearing just a loosely buttoned silk shirt, she tauntingly refutes his declarations of love:

> **Magda:** Have you had a girl?
> **Tomek:** No.
> **Magda:** When you watch me, do you do it with yourself?
> **Tomek:** I used to. Not now.
> **Magda:** I have nothing underneath. You know that, don't you? [Tomek nods.] When a woman wants a man, she becomes wet inside. I'm wet now.

Sitting before him, she takes his hands and makes him caress her thighs. Before his trembling fingers can even reach beneath the shirt, he emits a strangled yelp then hangs his head shamefully. 'Already?' she asks. His silent affirmation is utterly pathetic.

'That's all there is to love,' she says. 'Wash in the bathroom.'

Tomek's subsequent suicide attempt (he slits his wrists) is prolonged and difficult to watch, but nowhere near as painful as this scene of sexual humiliation.

Watching: voyeurism and pornography

Advertising for *Body Double* emphasizes its attention to voyeurism.

To describe *A Short Film About Love* as an East European *Rear Window* would be both simplistic and disingenuous. But so ingrained is Hitchcock's thriller in the collective movie-going consciousness that it is easy to overlook how demure his treatment (see chapter two) of the subject matter is.

Of Brian de Palma's Hitchcock homage **Body Double** (1984), the opposite is true. Combining elements of *Rear Window* and *Vertigo* (see chapter five), the plot is voyeuristic in the most absolutely sexual sense. B-movie actor Jake (Craig Wesson) finds himself out of work when his claustrophobia gets him fired from the set of a vampire movie (he goes into palpitations whenever there's a coffin scene), and homeless after he storms out of his girlfriend's apartment having caught her in a compromising position with another man.

He is befriended by Sam (Gregg Henry), a fellow thespian

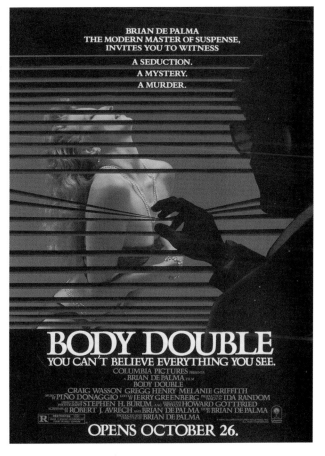

BRIAN DE PALMA
THE MODERN MASTER OF SUSPENSE, INVITES YOU TO WITNESS

A SEDUCTION.
A MYSTERY.
A MURDER.

BODY DOUBLE
YOU CAN'T BELIEVE EVERYTHING YOU SEE.

COLUMBIA PICTURES PRESENTS
A BRIAN DE PALMA FILM
BODY DOUBLE
CRAIG WASSON GREGG HENRY MELANIE GRIFFITH
MUSIC BY PINO DONAGGIO EDITED BY JERRY GREENBERG PRODUCTION DESIGNER IDA RANDOM
DIRECTOR OF PHOTOGRAPHY STEPHEN H. BURUM A.S.C. EXECUTIVE PRODUCER HOWARD GOTTFRIED
SCREENPLAY BY ROBERT J. AVRECH AND BRIAN DE PALMA STORY BY BRIAN DE PALMA
PRODUCED AND DIRECTED BY BRIAN DE PALMA

OPENS OCTOBER 26.

109

who is housesitting a swish Beverley Hills pad for an acquaintance on business in Europe. When Sam lands a role in an out-of-town production, he asks Jake to keep an eye on the house. With little else to occupy his time, Jake spends his evenings using Sam's telescope to spy on the house opposite where, each night, a dark-haired woman performs a seductive dance routine, before reclining on her bed and masturbating.

Jake also becomes aware of a man with a hideously disfigured face, a Native American, stalking her. Out of concern, he follows her himself. He learns her name: Gloria (Deborah Shelton). They almost become involved, but distrusting his motives, she flees. Later, Jake again watches her through the telescope. He sees the Native American break into her house and murder her with an electric drill. The police's only witness, he is soon under suspicion himself.

Proof that Jake has been played for a fool (proof also that he is a voyeur) comes when he watches a pornographic film and recognizes the dance routine he has seen performed over several evenings. In order to unravel the conspiracy (he is being set up to provide the police with a description of a suspect that will exonerate the actual perpetrator), Jake enters the business of pornographic film production in order to meet the 'actress' in question, the unsubtly named Holly Body (Melanie Griffith).

In a scene that might, in a more plausible narrative, have offered some indication of the depth of the protagonist's sexual obsession, Jake lands a supporting role in Holly's latest production. The voyeur is thus recast as exhibitionist, Jake tackling his big scene with Holly in fine, uninhibited style, not the least bit self-conscious at the presence of a camera crew. In fact, he gets so carried away that, much to Holly's surprise, he fails to adhere to the unwritten aesthetic of hardcore pornography and ejaculate onto his co-star, instead reaching climax while they are still locked in their embrace.

'Hey, what's he doing, *Last Tango*?' the cameraman demands: 'Where's the money shot?'

There is a similar moment in **Boogie Nights** (Paul Thomas Anderson, 1997), where the pornographic movie industry is portrayed as a microcosm of film production for the purposes of satirizing the traditional Hollywood 'rags to riches' narrative. Beginning in the late Seventies and spanning almost a decade, the soon-to-be-corrupted innocent whose rise and fall it charts is a 17-year-old working-class youth (Mark Wahlberg) whose only asset is a significant over-endowment in the penile department. Introduced to the world of hardcore film by director Jack Horner (Burt Reynolds), he re-invents himself as Dirk Diggler and becomes an overnight sensation, then loses himself in drugs and materialism.

His first starring role sees him paired with an actress called Amber Waves (Julianne Moore). The film proves to be a hilarious send-up of the shoddy production values and stilted dialogue typical of hardcore pornography. Footage of their coupling as seen through the lens is intercut with shots of the production crew, most of them looking bored, cigarettes dangling from their lips. Dirk and Amber's moans are accompanied by the clicking sound of film spooling through the camera. When the film runs out they are interrupted mid-coitus and asked to hold their position while the magazine is changed. Dirk and Amber exchange bland small talk while they wait. The changeover completed, they 'go at it' again. The whole enterprise is resolutely unerotic.

Amber, a seasoned performer, has behaved very protectively from the outset, aware that it's Dirk's first time in front of the camera (during the course of the film, her relationship with him becomes perversely maternal). As Dirk approaches climax, Amber breaks character:

Amber: Are you ready to come?
Dirk: Yes.
Amber: I want you to come in me.
Dirk: What?
Amber: It's all right, I'm fixed. I want you to come in me.

He obliges. The crew looks on, astounded. 'We missed the come shot,' production assistant Little Bill (William H Macy) complains. 'He came inside her. Maybe we can go to stock footage.'

'Are you crazy?' Horner responds, so affronted one would think he was directing something artistic. 'It won't match.'

As with *Body Double*, the purpose of this scene is to make the film safe for viewing by the mainstream market, where depiction of the world of hardcore movies is permissible as long as the 'money shot' is avoided.

Payment: sex as a commodity

While the milieu of pornographic movies – essentially a controlled form of prostitution where performers are paid to have sex with each other for the gratification of those who pay to see the film – is something most of *Boogie Nights'* characters recognize as a means to an end and ultimately want to move away from (one leaves to start his

Joe Buck (Jon Voight) makes the transition from gigolo to rent boy in *Midnight Cowboy*.

own business, another resumes her education), Joe Buck (Jon Voight), the almost painfully naive hero of John Schlesinger's ***Midnight Cowboy*** (1969), is open about his motivations from the outset. He leaves the hick little Texan town of his birth, bound for New York where it's his intent to cater to 'rich women willing to pay for it'. Joe Buck's aim in life is to be a gigolo; a hustler. The pre-credits sequence sees him leave his old life behind and swagger off to the big city with such cocksure bravado that one is tempted to believe he is his own man and sure to succeed.

Soon enough, however, a series of misadventures reveal that he is stunningly inept in his chosen profession. Twisted round her little finger by his first pick-up, he ends up giving her money. His sexuality is called into question as swiftly as his competence. Lodging, until his money runs out, in a hotel room, he decorates the walls with beefcake posters and spends a questionable amount of time posing shirtless in front of the mirror. Later, penniless, he moves into a dingy tenement with fellow loser 'Ratso' Rizzo (Dustin Hoffman), where they bicker like an old married couple.

Inevitably, rich women with a preference for rough trade prove few and far between and the hustler becomes a rent boy. It is during his first homosexual 'trick' that we learn the real reason behind his hasty departure from Texas. His client is a bespectacled student, the venue a cinema. Buck allows the youth to go down on him, forcing his mind away from the business at hand by conjuring images of his

112

former girlfriend, Annie (Jennifer Salt). This segues into another, less palatable, memory: he and Annie dragged from the backseat of a pick-up truck by a jeering mob, Buck forced to watch an assault against Annie, then anally raped himself.

This memory further throws into question Buck's decision to earn his living from the provision of sexual services. His transition from gigolo to rent boy is degrading enough; now we realize that both hetero- and homosexual activity are freighted with traumatic connotations.

The motives of Pierre (Daniel Auteuil) in **The Escort** (Michel Blanc, 1999) are ever cloudier than Buck's. Whereas Buck, subconsciously at least, becomes a hustler as a form of self-evasion, Pierre finds himself locked in a downward spiral whilst conning himself that he is on a voyage of self-discovery. A university lecturer in his forties, with a wife and teenage son, he responds to a mid-life crisis by walking out of his elegant Paris apartment and moving to a dingy rooming house in London where he tries to write a novel.

Running low on money and completely devoid of inspiration, he finds a wellspring of both in the lifestyle alternative offered to him by Tom (Stuart Townsend), whom he meets after a misadventure at a Soho club. A coffee-bar manager by day and professional escort (i.e. gigolo) in the evenings, Tom offers him work in the more legitimate (and less profitable) of his two enterprises. As the friendship between them develops, Tom has Pierre accompany him on an easy job: posing as boyfriends to a couple of society girls in order to hide their lesbian relationship from their respective parents. 'We didn't even have to fuck them,' Tom observes, responding to Pierre's moral concerns.

His qualms are quickly calmed. Tom gets him on the books of an agency and shows him the ropes. Pierre, after a hesitant first transaction, quickly develops a flair for the work; soon, he is murmuring French poetry to his clients during intercourse. Like Zorg in Betty Blue (see chapter two), he begins to live out his novel instead of writing it.

The nature of the job, of course, dictates that Pierre has to be able to perform sexually on demand. Sex, therefore, becomes functional. An act. Lack of emotional connection threatens to dehumanize him. He crosses the line with Patricia (Claire Skinner), who develops a need for him, which he later crassly exploits. Her vulnerability is brought into sharp contrast with his suave, insincere professional mannerism at their first appointment. Patricia lies on a hotel bed, a sheet covering her stomach and breasts. Her head is turned to one side, a look of unease on her face. 'At first I thought it just needed time,' she says, addressing someone offscreen, 'like it was all my fault. I never dared talk to him about it. I always pretended. In fact, I've been thinking about it for three months. I read an article about escorts where a woman said it had saved her marriage.'

The camera pans down to her raised legs. Pierre looks up (he is providing cunnilingus) and whispers, 'Relax. Everything's fine.'

Patricia makes eye contact with him for the first time, shocked that he clearly hasn't taken on board a thing she's said. 'I wouldn't want you to think badly of me,' she says reprovingly.

By the denouement, which sees him no less a sell-out for having written up his experiences as a best-selling novel (the last scene has the publisher's wife paying him for his services), he has edged into drugs, destroyed his relationship with his wife and son, compromised his friendship with Tom and led Patricia on with false assurances that she is more than just a client in order to glean more money from her.

As insalubrious as handing over cash for sexual services might be deemed, the incidents in *Midnight Cowboy* and *The Escort* are simple, businesslike transactions compared to the cynical scheme devised by the protagonists of **The Wings of the Dove** (Iain Softley, 1998). Kate Croy (Helena Bonham Carter), scion of an upper-class family, is threatened with disinheritance when she enters into a relationship with working-class journalist Merton Densher (Linus Roache). Although she wants to marry him, the borderline poverty of the lifestyle she would have to accept seems untenable. That is until she meets Milly Theale (Alison Elliott), an American heiress who, despite her youth and beauty, is in ill health. And, moreover, has no-one of her immediate acquaintance to whom she can leave her estate. Kate not only decides to manipulate her embryonic friendship with Milly, but also cajoles Merton into becoming involved with her.

The ensuing complication of friendships, loyalties and love is played out in the decaying grandeur of Venice (cf. *Don't Look Now* – see chapter two). After Milly's inevitable death, however, the scene shifts back to London. The endgame occurs at Merton's shabby flat, where he and Kate are alone with their shared guilt. Merton shows Kate an unopened letter from Milly's solicitors, confirmation of her bequests. Kate tosses it on the fire and leaves the room. After watching it burn for a moment or two, Merton follows her into the bedroom where she is sitting on the edge of his bed, undressing. They talk,

Merton suggesting they write to the solicitors, renouncing their claim to Milly's wealth. Kate undresses him and they lie together.

> **Merton**: I love you.
> **Kate:** I love you, too. [Pause] What are you thinking about? [He doesn't answer.] You're still in love with her.
> **Merton:** I was never in love with her.
> **Kate:** While she was alive, no.
> **Merton:** I'm sorry, Kate. I'm so sorry.
> **Kate:** It doesn't matter.

Kate moves on top of him and they begin making love. There is a palpable sense of desperation about the act. Kate breaks down and turns away. After a period of silence, Merton tells Kate he still wants to marry her, but on the condition that they live without Milly's wealth. Kate says she has a condition of her own: that Merton swears he is not in love with Milly's memory. Merton cannot answer and Kate leaves.

That the sexual act is not completed speaks for itself. That the entire scene plays out while they are naked is crucial. In a film about betrayal and deceit, it is emblematic of the openness and naked emotionalism that has been too late in occurring between them. Also, given that *The Wings of the Dove* is a costume drama (adapted from the novel by Henry James), it is notable that its denouement sees the period costumes (and by extension the vapid prettiness that afflicts many such productions) stripped away.

In this respect, *The Wings of the Dove* can be seen to have an antecedent in Jane Campion's Oscar-winning **The Piano** (1993). Again, the usually prettified ethos of the costume drama is rendered as dark and murky as the moral choices faced by its protagonist, Ada McGrath (Holly Hunter). A mute Irishwoman, she is sold by her father as a bride to New Zealand landowner Stewart (Sam Neill). She makes the voyage overseas with her young daughter Flora (Anna Paquin) and her beloved piano. Things turn unpleasant from the outset: her new home is a muddy, rainswept plantation where facilities are basic to say the least. Stewart refuses to have her piano hauled up from the beach; and – worse – when his half-Maori neighbour Baines (Harvey Keitel) professes an interest in music, gives it over to him in exchange for a plot of land. To add insult to injury, Stewart insists that Ada visit Baines to give him lessons.

Baines's motives soon become apparent. He has no interest in learning the instrument. Instead, he offers Ada the chance to earn it back, a key at a time. As he puts it, in the film's most memorable line, 'There's things I'd like to do while you play.' The nature of Baines's requests alters from lesson to lesson. 'Lift your skirt,' he instructs at an early session, 'lift it higher' – this done, he crawls under the piano and touches her skin through a hole in her stockings. Later, he tells her 'undo your dress, I want to see your arms'. She undresses to her corset and continues playing.

Ada's compliance with Baines is contrasted with the lack of sex in her relationship with Stewart. Unattracted to him, she rejects his advances. Stewart's cloying, almost effeminate personality – he mopes around, whining that 'one day [Ada] might come to feel something for me' – is at odds with Baines's rough sexuality. Ada's attraction to him develops. At another session, she breaks off playing to find Baines standing by his bed, naked. 'I want to lie together without clothes on,' he says directly. 'How many would that be?' They agree on 10 keys. Ada disrobes and lies with Baines; their closeness quickly leads to lovemaking. Afterwards, Baines is remorseful. 'This arrangement's making you a whore,' he realizes. He returns the piano to her.

Events take another turn when she returns to him willingly, only for their affair to be discovered by Stewart, who extracts a brutal revenge on her. Resolutely downbeat – even the closing scenes, which see Ada and Baines reunited, are staged so ambiguously that they can be taken as Ada's dying fantasy – *The Piano* subverts all the expectations/clichés of the genre and presents an examination of sexual passion that is refreshingly free of judgementalism. After all, are the actions of Baines – who is genuinely attracted to Ada and at least expresses regret at the way he orchestrated their 'arrangement' – any more questionable that those of Stewart, who treats her as little more than property?

S/M: pain and power

Given the success of *Emmanuelle* (see chapter two), it was inevitable that Just Jaeckin's follow-up would tread a similar path: soft-core, soft-focus, heavy emphasis on sexual power games. But whereas Emmanuelle embarks upon a journey of sexual self-discovery, the heroine of **The Story of O** (1975) subjugates herself to the fantasies of others. The depersonalization she allows herself to be put through begins with her name: throughout the film she is referred to only as O.

Taken by her boyfriend René (Jean Gaven) to an isolated chateau, O (Corinne Cleary) is discharged into the dubious care of two women, their breasts exposed but otherwise fully clothed, who undress her, comb her hair and apply make-up and fix a collar round her neck. They then lead her into a large room filled with leering men and a number of women (all similarly outfitted in the accoutrements of bondage). She is admired, groped, sodomized by one of the men and forced to fellate another. 'I want to hear her scream,' one of her tormentors decides, at which point Jaeckin introduces the film's key image: O, naked and bound, being whipped. It is an image he revisits with interminable monotony.

The above described occupies merely the first 10 minutes. No effort has been made to introduce the characters, analyze their relationship, or explain why O is so complicit in these atrocities. Having passed out from the whipping, she is awoken by René; their brief conversation gives some indication of her mindset.

> **O:** You see. I managed to stand it.
> **René:** You did well.
> **O:** For you, René.

What this exchange does not achieve, however, is any explanation of why she feels compelled to give herself up to these misuses for René's sake. The voice-over – large passages of purple prose from the film's source material, a novel by Pauline Réage – offers such negligible insights as 'O wondered why there was so much sweetness mingled with her terror, or why she found her terror so delicious'. Such evasions leave the filmmakers unjustified in their sequence of salacious set-pieces, which essentially amount to more of the same, with O whipped, sexually humiliated and passed from one abusive partner to another for the next hour and a half.

Michael Haneke's **_The Piano Teacher_** (2001) occupies the more intelligent and psychologically acute end of the spectrum. Erika Kohut (Isabelle Huppert) is driven to extreme behaviour by sexual repression, a condition that owes to the malign influence of her domineering mother (Annie Girardot). An instructor at the Vienna Conservatory, Erika still lives with her mother – still shares a bedroom with her – despite being in her late thirties. She dresses in a manner that is almost androgynous, and seems to display no emotion. She is unduly harsh towards her students. The outlets she finds make for uncomfortable viewing. In an early scene she visits a sex shop, where she pays for a private booth. Here, a split screen on a video monitor offers trailers for four different hardcore productions (a device by which Haneke introduces actual footage of fellatio and penetration into the narrative of his film). Having made her choice, she reaches forward into a waste bin located beneath the screen and retrieves a crumpled tissue (evidently provided by the proprietors for the purposes of post-onanistic personal hygiene), which she then holds to her nose. Haneke allows his camera to record this unsavoury moment for a full 25 seconds.

Equally dispassionate – and almost unwatchable – is the depiction of her act of self-mutilation later in the film. She sits on the edge of her bath (the bathroom suite is a clinical white), naked apart from a robe, a mirror angled between her legs as she applies a disposable razor to her genitals. The camera never moves; there is not a single cutaway. A thin line of blood rolls down the side of the bath as her mother's nasal tones call demandingly from the other side of the bathroom door.

Worse is the way that Erika attempts to rope her student, Walter Klemmer (Benoît Magimel), into her masochism. Realizing he is attracted to her, she instigates a series of sexual power games with him. Refusing to make love with him in the normal sense of the term, she insists on controlling the situation. She informs him he will receive her 'instructions'. He does, by letter, and discovers that the control issue has been turned on its head. Her letter is little more than a catalogue of sadomasochistic fantasies. 'Give me lots of slaps,' she writes, in one of the more restrained passages: 'hit me around the face and hit me hard.'

Frustrated, torn between his attraction to her and what he sees as her 'sickness', Walter visits her at home and confronts her. The situation is intensified by Erika's mother, whom Walter finally manhandles into a spare room and locks her in. Anger pushes him over the line. He slaps Erika across the face. Hard. Twice. 'Is this how you imagined it?' he demands, knocking her to the floor with another blow, then delivering a kick to the face, hard enough to make her bleed.

At this point, both have transgressed even the most liberal standards of normality. Walter at least attempts some form of atonement, treating her tenderly thereafter. Not that this counts for much. He tries to make love to her normally (which, in as much defence as one can muster for him at this point, is all he has wanted from the outset), but she remains entirely unresponsive. Eventually, he desists and takes his leave.

That Haneke shifts the focus onto Walter at this point (having structured the entire film thus far as a character study of Erika), and moreover that he allows Walter the audience-pleasing act of finally dealing with Erika's mother, is arguably indicative that, in the final analysis, *The Piano Teacher* remains the work of a male director. It is interesting to compare the film with Catherine Breillat's no less controversial **Romance** (1999), which also includes scenes of onscreen penetration and fellatio. Here, the main character, Marie (Caroline Ducey), is not driven by repression; instead, her actions are a response to the sexual hang-ups of her partner, Paul (Sagamore Stevenin), who – for some unexplained reason – rejects her need for intimacy, objects to her touching his penis, and only agrees to intercourse as a 'duty call' (i.e. at her optimal time in order to effect pregnancy).

Although she professes love for him (indeed, one wonders why she stays with such an emotionally challenged individual; even when she does conceive, towards the end of the film, he starts drinking heavily rather than face up to his responsibilities), she seeks sexual gratification with other men. The first is Paolo (Rocco Siffredi)[1], a hunky Italian who has been celibate for several months following his girlfriend's death in a car accident. He responds to Marie's advances, providing the no-strings-attached physical act that she requires.

Soon, however, she meets Robert (François Berléand), an older man who collects bondage equipment and claims that he has made over 10,000 conquests. Unlike Paolo, he doesn't wait till consent has been offered. Without the slightest attempt at foreplay, without even a pretence of romanticism, he calmly offers a running commentary on the situation as his hand moves between her legs: 'You're amazed that I'm fingering your pussy, but it's me doing it. I'm not aroused yet, but you are … That's the way it goes. Beautiful women are taken by ugly men. That's a well-kept secret. There has to be action, and the action isn't between man and woman – that's too simple. It's between beauty and ugliness. Beauty feeds on degradation … That's where I come in.' This is not seduction; it is merely statement of fact.

In Robert she finds a kindred spirit. An ersatz relationship develops between them. (In a truly bizarre moment, Robert is present at the birth of her child, even as Paul dies in a gas explosion, which she has engineered.) Robert has the least orthodox sexual tastes of any of the male characters, but it is he who comforts Marie when she has a bad experience, he who tailors their bondage sessions to her wants ('you tie me up without tying me down' as she puts it).

Marie is by no means an entirely sympathetic character – her opinions are contradictory, often hypocritical ('I can cheat on you,' she tells Paul, 'but you can't cheat on me'); and her orchestration of his death is as cold-blooded as it is needless – but in the hands of a female director, the issue becomes that of her right: not just to do, but to have done to her. *Romance* is a difficult, thought-provoking film, but very focused; in fact, its only non sequitur is its title.

Obsession and self-destruction

If audiences in the mid-Seventies reeled from *Ai No Corrida* (see chapter two), a study of obsessive sexual behaviour, it was not for want of being unprepared. Two years before Oshima's film was released, Liliana Cavani's **The Night Porter** (1974) outraged audiences with a similar story – two lovers locked in the mutually destructive bonds of a claustrophobic and decidedly unhealthy relationship – played out under the dark shadow of Nazism.

The film takes its title from the job Max (Dirk Bogarde) holds down at a Vienna hotel; a tedious job, but effectively low profile. And Max, the commandant of a concentration camp during the war, is keen not to be recognized. His only social activities are secret meetings with former colleagues (they hold mock trials for each other) and the occasional evening at the opera. Perverse as the former might be, it's the latter that proves his undoing. At a performance of Mozart's *Die Zauberflöte* he encounters Lucia (Charlotte Rampling), wife of a renowned conductor. She recognizes him as the man who, years before (the film is set in 1957), was not just her captor but also her lover. She broods over the nature of their relationship: she the submissive, the sexual plaything; he the tyrant, the dominator. They agree to meet, Max fearing that she will turn him over to the authorities. Quite the opposite. She wants their relationship to resume: the only difference is that this time her subjugation is 'of my own free will'.

With supreme irony, both end up prisoners in Max's apartment. With police combing Vienna for Lucia at her husband's insistence, Max's colleagues worry about the heat this could bring on them. They stake out the apartment and prevent supplies of food being taken in. Finally, with Max and Lucia worn down and unresistant, they kidnap them, driving them to an isolated spot and executing them.

Predictably, the film caused outrage. Three decades on, it still disturbs. What is truly chilling, though, is that the genesis of Cavani's narrative was factual. Filming a documentary at Dachau, Cavani witnessed a woman laying a spread of roses on the ground. The site was where she had been imprisoned. The roses were to honour the memory, not of a relative or fellow prisoner, but the Nazi officer she had had an affair with who had been shot by Americans when the camp was liberated.

As the basis for a film (Cavani was spurred on by wondering what would have happened if the officer *hadn't* been shot and the two met again, years later), it's as controversial as a scenario can be. Feminists, Nazi survivors and Jewish communities the world over were united in outcry. One can only imagine how deeper the offence would have been to the latter had Lucia been portrayed in her erstwhile incarnation: Bogarde, in his autobiography *An Orderly Man*, recalls that in the first draft of the script, the character was Jewish. In the completed film, she is sent to the camp because of her family's Socialist politics. She is young (Rampling's delicate, somewhat androgynous looks are used to startling effect), pliable to Max's whims. He calls her 'my little girl'. Not that his intentions are in any way fatherly. In the film's most provocative image, seized upon for the poster artwork, he exerts his sexual control of her by having her parade in front of the other officers dressed only in trousers, a pair of braces, leather gloves and a Nazi cap. Costume has seldom been used in film to make a more perverse erotic statement. There is a theatricality to her enforced performance (one thinks of the emotionless, robotic movements of a catwalk model) that leaves no doubt that Lucia is being objectified, which gives the Fifties-set section of the film an even darker tone. We see the same story being played out twice: the first time around, she has no choice; the second, she acts of her own volition. Ultimately, both she and Max pay the price for their twisted sexual dependence on each other, but the fact that they are executed by unremorseful Nazis doesn't even allow for a moral quality to their demise[2].

Questions of identity and wartime allegiances are very much to the fore in **The Beguiled** (Don Siegel, 1970), which sees the repressed sexual hysteria of Black Narcissus (see chapter one) relocated to the American Civil War. The setting is a seminary for young ladies run by Martha Farnsworth (Geraldine Page). Martha is a case study in repression: she has had an incestuous relationship with her now deceased brother (his death is never accounted for), and harbours a lesbian attraction to one of her staff, Edwina (Elizabeth Hartman). Both are jealous of the wanton good looks of 17-year-old student Carol (Jo Ann Harris).

Into this tense environment, already riddled with petty jealousies and power plays, comes wounded Union soldier John McBurney (Clint Eastwood). The girls and women nurse him back to health, intending to turn him over to a Confederate patrol as soon as possible. Initially out of self-preservation, he worms his way into their affections, lying about his role in the military (he claims to be a Quaker, attached to his regiment purely to tend to the injured – a flashback reveals him as a regular soldier, shooting his enemy without hesitation).

He is soon playing Martha, Edwina and Carol off against each other. He exploits Martha's sexual confusion, making intermittent guarded comments, which he allows her to construe as overtures. He flatters the virginal Edwina, encouraging her to be more open in her self-expression. Carol takes no work at all: she all but offers herself to him from the outset.

The eternal triangle is one thing – this is more like a quadrangle. And all points of it converge during an elliptically edited fantasy sequence. Three divergent points of view are established: McBurney's as he lies in his room, flashbacks demonstrating that he is thinking about the intimate moments he has so far shared with all three women; Martha's as she lays out her nightgown on her bed, her hair loose and falling around her shoulders (the first time in the film she looks anything other than a stern schoolma'am); and Edwina's as she undresses in her room, prior to turning in for the night. Through a series of superimpositions, Siegel segues into the fantasy sequence: McBurney enters Martha's room and begins making love to her; suddenly he turns away and the camera pulls back to reveal Edwina lying next to him. Jointly, Martha and Edwina turn their attentions to McBurney, pausing momentarily to share a lesbian kiss.

Siegel never fully reveals whose fantasy this is, although it's certainly not McBurney's – he is very shortly seen enjoying Carol's favours. The lesbian element points to Martha. However, the fantasy sequence is curtailed when Edwina, alerted by sounds from the room above, discovers McBurney and Carol in the act. It is at this point, as with Sister Ruth in *Black Narcissus*, that sexual repression tips over into violence. Edwina attacks McBurney with a candlestick, knocking him downstairs. In an act of vengeance, the women amputate his injured leg. Later, when he tries to reassert his masculinity, winning over Edwina (whom he intends to use as a way out of what has essentially become his prison), the others conspire to poison him.

Jealousy – in this case imagined – is also the motivation behind the sexual misadventures of social-climbing physician Dr Bill Harford (Tom Cruise) – a Nineties update of Pierre in *Belle de Jour* (see chapter three) – in Stanley Kubrick's **Eyes Wide Shut** (1999). Self-confident to the point that he takes everything in life for granted, Harford's preconceptions are shaken when, during an argument with his wife Alice (Nicole Kidman), she admits she has fantasized about another man – a man she considered leaving him for. Before the argument can be resolved, Harford receives a call informing him a patient has died. He uses this as an excuse to leave the house, and goes out into the night. Kubrick structures the first half of the film around his misadventures from hereon in, and the second on the consequences – both actual and potential.

He is propositioned by the daughter of the deceased patient, but turns her down. He is enticed back to the apartment of a hooker, but leaves without doing the deed after he receives a call from Alice on his mobile (a wise decision – we learn in a later scene that she has tested HIV positive). He experiences a surreal episode at a fancy dress shop, whose proprietor is pimping his underage daughter, and leaves in disgust when her services are offered to him.

But the centrepiece of Harford's nocturnal perambulations – throughout which he is tormented by visions of Alice having sex with another man, an imagined act of unfaithfulness – is the 18-minute 'Fidelio'[3] scene. Harford meets an old friend, the wonderfully named Nick Nightingale (Todd Field), a medical student turned jazz pianist. Nightingale describes a series of private functions he has played at, where he has been obliged to play blindfolded. 'Last time the blindfold wasn't on so well,' he says; 'I have seen one or two things in my life, but never anything like this. And never such women.'

Harford inveigles the location and password of that evening's function from him, acquires the requisite costume (tuxedo, cape, mask), and attends. What ensues resembles a Masonic ritual re-imagined by Hugh Hefner. A dozen masked and cloaked figures stand in a circle. At the centre, an individual dressed like a high-priest delivers a monotonous incantation in Latin while he swings an incense-filled orb. Simultaneously, the cloaked figures divest themselves of said cloaks. All are women: statuesque; naked but for G-strings and their masks. All participants remain masked for the duration.

Such dramatic tension as the scene generates owes to how soon Harford's identity will be discovered (he is twice exhorted to leave while he still can by one of the women). Following their disrobement, the women are placed at the service of the men in attendance, most of whom seem more interested in watching sexual acts than participating. Harford walks from room to room, looking: he, too, is more aroused by the voyeuristic aspects. Accordingly, what he sees is less an orgy (one can imagine the Marquis de Sade finding it all too polite, making his excuses and leaving) than a series of tableaux: two women locked in a 69 position, attended by a group of men, studying them as if a medical experiment were taking place; a lesbian threesome, the participants so indifferent they resemble little more than objects posed for a still life; a man mechanically and joylessly copulating with a woman as she reclines on a human table, a masked flunkey kneeling on all fours to fulfil this role.

Ultimately, the 'Fidelio' scene serves two functions: it provides the pinnacle (or nadir, depending upon one's perspective) of Harford's long dark night of the libido, taking him to a place he truly should not have been (later, he is intimidated into keeping silent about what he has seen). It is also a vision of sex without intimacy, without love – cold, anonymous, impersonal. It represents what Harford stands to lose. As warped as his sexual musings have become by this point, he does at least regain perspective; the film ends with him determining to hold on to his family above all else.

There isn't even this small glimmer of affirmation in Mike Figgis's **Leaving Las Vegas** (1995). An essay in self-destruction, its 15-minute pre-credits sequence has Ben Sanderson (Nicolas Cage) drink himself out of a profitable job with a Hollywood studio, make an embarrassment of himself in numerous bars and strip clubs, burn his possessions and depart LA for the even less salubrious climes of

Las Vegas. His reasons for alcoholism are predictable: his wife has left him; he is disaffected with his job (when someone compliments him on a screenplay, his caustic response is 'I didn't write it, I just took credit').

On arrival in Las Vegas, he works out a plan of campaign: five weeks to drink himself to death, budgeting $200–$300 per day, with the occasional luxury. The luxury in question being high-class hooker Sera (Elisabeth Shue). It is Sera who gives the film its emotional core, offsetting Ben's suave, witty nihilism. The narrative is punctuated by her addresses to camera, staged as if the audience were an off-screen therapist, during which she details the degradations of her profession. An example: 'He was so proud of his large erection … He started pounding me, really hard. I remember I had to bite my tongue to keep from crying … He said, "I'm going to come on your face." He rubbed the semen all over my face and in my hair. Then he kicked me off the bed and told me to leave.'

This incident is recounted early in the film, before she meets Ben, and the rampant priapism of her nameless client is an effective counterpoint to the impotence Ben suffers as a result of his drinking, something that becomes evident during their first encounter. At this point, they are merely hooker and client, but when Ben is unable to perform, later admitting that he didn't pick her up for sex but just wanted to talk, Sera recognizes something in him – something wounded and sensitive – that sets him apart from her typical 'dates'.

A relationship develops between them. Working freelance after her Latvian pimp Yuri (Julian Sands) is executed by a group of mob types after a business deal goes sour, she invites Ben to move in with her. The joint stipulation is that she will tolerate his drinking as long as he tolerates her profession. For a while the arrangement works. Until Sera betrays him by begging him to see a doctor, in response to which he lets her find him with another hooker. She throws him out.

By the end of the film, they are reconciled, though. Sera has suffered further abuses (including a particularly nasty gang rape by a bunch of college football jocks); Ben is on his deathbed. She visits him in his grubby hotel room. 'Do you want me to help you?' she asks, knowing his time is nearly up. He nods in affirmation. She coaxes him to erection then straddles him. For all that he swears his affection for her, what occurs is as much an act of leave-taking as an act of love. Sex as valediction. He cries as he climaxes. As she sleeps on his shoulder afterwards, he turns his head to look upon her one last time.

Then dies.

Like *Leaving Las Vegas*, Marco Ferreri's **Tales of Ordinary Madness** (1981) is essentially a perverse love story between an alcoholic writer and a prostitute. The writer here is Charles Serkin (Ben Gazzara), a thinly fictionalized Charles Bukowski, on whose verbosely titled autobiographical work *Erections, Ejaculations, Exhibitions and General Tales of Ordinary Madness* the film is based. A hangover from the days of beatniks, Serkin flits from woman to woman as

Hooker and alcoholic writer: Ornella Muti and Ben Gazzara in *Tales of Ordinary Madness*.

regularly as he stumbles from bar to bar. And it is in a typically seedy dive that he meets Cass (Ornella Muti). Her melancholy beauty appeals to him, but he is unprepared for her propensity for self-harm.

When he first takes her back to his minimally furnished room (a true poet, he starves and scribbles in his dingy garret), he lets her sleep while he works rather than cajole her into sex immediately. The following morning, he wakes to find her standing at the window, gazing out across the city, naked from the waist down. This is all Serkin needs by way of invitation, and he takes her from behind. He speaks one word as he reaches orgasm: 'Love.'

It is a moment she reminds him of later in the film. Finding her too intense, he has swanned off to enjoy the pleasures of other women. A brief reconciliation is then effected, Cass moving back into Serkin's room, but immediately she fears losing him again when he is offered a residence in New York. 'Love, you said,' she muses, lying on his bed, pale, her eyes unfocused, her words murmured as if from a faraway place; 'You made me forget. I'll always remember that.'

Sensing something is wrong (he is already aware that Cass has made suicide attempts), he throws back the bedsheet. There is blood on her nightdress.

Serkin: Oh my God. Oh my God. What the fuck did you do to yourself?
Cass: I've closed it. For you and for everybody. Forever.

126

Serkin reaches between her legs and removes the item she has used on herself: a large safety pin. (Mercifully, this is not dwelt upon or shown in detail.) If the gang rape in *Leaving Las Vegas* stands as Figgis's most graphic statement on the abuses Sera suffers in her line of work, this scene of genital mutilation is every bit as powerful in communicating the depersonalization and sexual objectification to which Cass has been subjected.

Alfred Hitchcock's **Marnie** (1964) may not feature such visceral imagery but it still ventures into dark territory, imposing upon its eponymous heroine the sexual obsessions of its director. Marnie Edgar (Tippi Hedren) is introduced in the very first shot, absconding with illegally acquired funds (cf. Janet Leigh in *Psycho*), wearing a black wig. Hitchcock loses no time in remodelling her as a blonde and building a warped romantic fantasy around her.

Adopting a new disguise and an assumed name, she wangles a job at a firm run by the charismatic and successful Mark Rutland (Sean Connery). Unattached since the death of his wife, Rutland finds himself attracted to her. Despite the advantages – Rutland is young, handsome and wealthy – she remains reticent. One evening she stages a robbery and disappears. Rutland tracks her down. With evidence against her, he manipulates the situation to his own ends, essentially blackmailing her into marrying him.

False comfort: the ruthless playboy and his frigid wife in Hitchcock's *Marnie*.

127

Rutland's attempts to have a normal relationship with her (notwithstanding the questionable means by which he instigated said relationship) are complicated by some repressed experience in childhood which leaves Marnie repulsed by the sexual advances of men. This tests Rutland's patience to the extreme on their honeymoon. Initially, he tries to understand her 'condition', but his concern is met with disdain and the insistence that they sleep apart.

> **Marnie:** If you don't want to go to bed, please get out.
> **Rutland:** But I do want to go to bed, Marnie. I very much want to go to bed. [He advances on her.]
> **Marnie:** No!

He tears the nightgown from her shoulders: in typically coy Hollywood fashion, it falls around her feet in a pool of silk; the shots of Marnie that follow are strictly head-and-shoulders. She stands, unblinking, unmoving, paralyzed by fear. Rutland hesitates, then divests himself of his dressing gown and drapes it around her, apologizing. But Hitchcock isn't content to let the audience off so lightly. Rutland becomes very tactile, very gentle, sitting her down on the edge of the bed – then he forces himself on her, eyes cold with dark intent as he looms over her, his face filling the screen.

Adapted from Winston Graham's novel by Jay Presson Allen, early drafts of the script were written by Evan Hunter, who had provided the screenplay for *The Birds* (1963). Hunter, however, found the rape scene unnecessary and lobbied Hitchcock not to include it. The director was adamant. Eventually, Hunter was removed from the project and a new writer brought on board. As he recalls in his memoir *Me and Hitch*, 'many years later, when I told Jay Presson Allen how much [Hitchcock's] description of that scene had bothered me, she said, "You just got bothered by the scene that was his reason for making the movie …" '[4].

In direct contrast to *Marnie*, where frigidity is the result of trauma, sexual abandonment as a catharsis for grief is the theme of Carine Adler's debut film **Under the Skin** (1997), winner of the Edinburgh Film Festival's Michael Powell Award. The opening scenes sketch out the unspoken rivalry between sisters Iris (Samantha Morton) and Rose (Claire Rushbrook). Rose is married, pregnant, and maintaining a balance between her home life and her career. She is emblematic of 'all that love and marriage and Christmas tree shit' that Iris rails against.

But if Rose is just too picture-perfect, then Iris borders on the unstable. She is temperamental, immature, quick to take offence and has a clingingly obsessive relationship with her boyfriend, her behaviour eventually driving him to an affair with her best friend Vron (Christine Tremarco). The volatile relationship between Iris and Rose is tested to its limits when their mother (Rita Tushingham) dies shortly after being diagnosed with a terminal illness.

Rose has plenty to cling on to – both emotionally and materially – in order to get through the grieving process. Iris, however, has split up with her boyfriend, quit her dead-end job and found herself alone in a nondescript flat. She searches for meaning in the purely physical. Clad in her mother's wig and fur coat, she goes looking for easy sex; and whenever this fails, she masturbates with an equal degree of desperation.

Iris's psychology is writ large (as a replacement for the affection she believes her mother never quite gave her, favouring Rose instead, she uses props belonging to her mother as a disguise – an emotional barrier – while she seeks physical gratification as a substitute for emotional fulfilment), Adler decisively depicting the confused mindset of her character. Iris's first sexual encounter, shortly after her mother's funeral, is with Tom (Stuart Townsend), a man she meets at a cinema. As they talk after the film, their dialogue fades out, replaced by Iris's recollections after the event, delivered in voice-over. Her tone is dispassionate, almost philosophical: 'I don't know why I went up to this man, maybe it was his eyes, the sound of his voice, or the way he moved … I wanted to kiss him, and so I did.' At this point the voice-over segues from past to present tense, indicating the immediacy of the act. 'I slide my thigh between his legs. He lifts up my skirt … He kisses my breasts, my stomach … He stands behind me, his hands on my hips … his hand between my legs, parting me … .'

A montage of shots accompanies this soliloquy, inter-cutting Iris and Tom's lovemaking with the funeral and cremation of Iris's mother. Thus the film from the outset (this scene occurs approximately quarter of an hour into the running time) interlinks its thematic concerns: sex and death. Rose's pregnancy emphasizes this idea of the loss of a life measured against the continuation of life in general.

Under the Skin is also notable for the strong sexual self-identity of its heroine. Whereas many films containing multiple scenes of sexual imagery portray the female partners in these encounters as little more than ciphers, the opposite is true here. The men Iris picks up are objectified: they have little personality, are afforded no history and are not dwelled upon. As with the double flashback of the scene with Tom – to their night together, and during that to the funeral – the viewer has the sense of being twice-removed from the male partner. Therefore, empathy with Iris is total as her grief – and the behavioural tendencies in which it manifests itself – threatens to overwhelm her.

The basic scenario of **Breaking the Waves** (Lars von Trier, 1996) is similar – a mentally unstable heroine; obsessiveness exacerbated by a personal tragedy – but the implications are darker, the outcome bleaker. Whereas Iris emerges more or less unscathed from her misadventures and manages to reconcile with her sister, von Trier's tragic heroine, Bess McNeill (Emily Watson), gives her life for a misguided sense of guilt borne of love and perverted by religion.

Set in the Seventies in a small village on the north-west coast of Scotland, von Trier establishes from the outset a stoic community whose dedication to the church is motivated more by fear than love. An early scene has a former parishioner, since banished from the fold, buried in unconsecrated ground: 'You are a sinner,' the priest intones, 'and for your sins will burn in Hell.' Later, as Bess's behaviour becomes increasingly erratic, her mother warns her that she risks similarly being exiled: 'I've seen strong people wither after being cast out.' Even at her wedding, a query as to why no bells are rung after the service is answered with a stern 'we have no bells – we do not need to be called to worship'.

Bess's take on religion is almost childlike. She conducts 'conversations' with God, answering herself in a deep voice. Her emotional volatility is worsened shortly after her marriage to Jan (Stellan Skarsgård), a roustabout on the oil-rig off the coast. Unhappy at his return to the rig after their all-too-brief honeymoon, she prays that he might be sent back to her. A freak accident occurs and he is helicoptered back to the mainland, paralyzed. Blaming herself, Bess seeks to make expiation. Inadvertently, it is Jan who sets her on the road to self-destruction.

Bed-ridden, unable to move, let alone perform sexually, Jan encourages Bess to find another man. Appalled, she refuses. His motives may be honourable – he is convinced he can no longer be a husband to her, and is distressed at her unhappiness – but his *modus operandi* is open to question. He tells her to have sex with other men, then return to the hospital and recount her exploits. 'It'll be like we're together,' he says. She takes him at his word, and makes advances to Dr Richardson (Adrian Rawlins), the sympathetic surgeon who is tending to Jan. Richardson declines her offer, and Bess embarks on a series of encounters with the few pitiful specimens of manhood the small community has to offer: she masturbates a doughy-faced old-timer on a bus ride across the gorse land; dresses like a hooker to draw attention to herself; allows herself to be picked up in a dingy bar by a portly middle-aged drinker (he takes her roughly in the lee of the church); and finally – and fatally – asks to be ferried out to a Russian freighter moored off the coast, despite warnings that 'none of the other girls' (i.e. the prostitutes who work the harbour) will attend the vessel. Once on board, two sailors, armed with gun and knife, brutalize her. Barely half alive, she is taken back to the mainland on a police launch and hospitalized.

As Bess wanes, then dies, Jan's condition improves. Coincidence or miracle? Von Trier comes out in favour of the latter in a finale that subverts the pathos and dourness of that which has preceded it. Rescuing her from internment in unconsecrated land, Jan's comrades steal Bess's coffin and effect a burial at sea. Later, miles out to sea and with nothing on the radar, they are perplexed by the sound of bells ringing. A cut to a high-angle shot (God's POV?) shows two large cast-iron bells, suspended in the ether.

So emotive is this metaphysical pay-off that one can easily be distracted from the dark implications von Trier is making (the pointless death of a deluded innocent is effectively legitimized as a form of martyrdom). Still, the film is notable for the interconnections it draws between sexuality, guilt and religion, a theme considered in further detail in chapter five.

Sex and death: the horror genre

If her sexuality is something Bess is seen to 'pay' for in *Breaking the Waves*, no matter that she is as much misled by her husband as by her own misconceptions vis-à-vis religion, then sexual activity in the horror movie is virtually a guarantee of a swift and bloody demise. The genre has always found its core fanbase in a younger audience – mid-teens to early-twenties – and its characters and settings generally mirror this demographic. Films such as *Halloween* (John Carpenter, 1978), *Friday the 13th* (Sean S Cunningham, 1980) and *Prom*

Night (Paul Lynch, 1980) established a trend for stalk-and-slash thrillers, based around high schools or (in the case of *Friday the 13th*) summer camps, and populated by teenagers. Sex is inevitably a prelude to death. At a stretch, one can make a case for this: loss of virginity = transition to adulthood[5]; adulthood = inevitability of mortality. However, the genre soon became so formulaic, and this aspect of it so prurient, that degeneracy into cliché was inevitable. 'You can never have sex, it's one of the rules' – so goes one of the most memorable lines in Wes Craven's *Scream* (1996), an effective satire on the conventions of the horror film. After *Scream*, it should have been impossible to revisit this milieu in anything less than the most ironic terms.

John Fawcett's **Ginger Snaps** (2000), however, evades all trace of cliché or banality, and does something new, even though he takes as his starting point one of horror's most hackneyed stock-in-trade industry standards, the werewolf[6]. It is into the lives of two teenage sisters, Ginger (Katharine Isabelle) and Brigitte Fitzgerald (Emily Perkins), that said lycanthrope intrudes. Both are cynical, world-hating goths, pariahs on campus and rebels in the family home. Their shared hobby is staging mock suicides. When Ginger is attacked and bitten, it coincides with her first period.

Fawcett and scriptwriter Karen Walton's stroke of genius is in equating Ginger's biological/hormonal changes with the increasingly lupine characteristics she takes on. Completely throwing out the rule book as regards swift human-to-wolf transitions brought on by the full moon, the filmmakers have Ginger effect her change incrementally. Moreover, the more wolf-like her appearance and behaviour, the more strikingly attractive she becomes, and the more sexually dangerous.

Breaking her pact with Brigitte that high-school boys are worthless and their bond as sisters transcends all else, Ginger becomes involved with football jock Jason (Jesse Moss). To say she loses her virginity to him would be a misrepresentation of the balance of power. Archetypal of such teenage trysts, the act occurs in the back seat of Jason's battered second-hand car. Ginger is the aggressor from the outset, something Jason is disconcerted by.

Jason: Take it easy. We've got all night ... Just lie back and relax.
Ginger: You lie back and relax.

Jason: Hey, who's the guy?

Ginger: Who's the guy here? [She pushes him backwards and straddles him.] Who's the fucking guy here?

Jason burbles helplessly about protection, begging her to stop. But Ginger has the upper hand. Shocked that she is stronger, he is forced to accede the dominant position. 'You're fucking right to be scared, boy,' she tells him. Her head disappears out of the frame as she descends on him. There is the sound of bite wounds being inflicted.

What we have here, then, is not only a direct equation of sex and horror (Ginger returns home afterwards, covered in blood, and tells Brigitte 'I get this ache – I thought it was for sex, but it's to tear everything to fucking pieces'), but the ethos of female sexuality, once freely expressed, as capable of unleashing destructive forces (see chapter one) transposed to a genre where the male is usually the sexual predator.

Of course, when one moves outside of the teenage demographic, the subject of sex in the horror film becomes less simplistic. Horny college types desperate to get their rocks off (even at the cost of victimhood to Freddie/Jason/Michael/whomever) is one thing, but the fate that befalls Sergeant Neil Howie (Edward Woodward) in **The Wicker Man** (Robin Hardy, 1973) is quite something else.

Temptation personified: Britt Ekland as the seductive Willow in *The Wicker Man.*

Arriving at Summerisle, a small Scottish island, to follow up reports of a schoolgirl's disappearance, Howie is horrified to discover that paganism and fertility rites are freely performed in the community and taught at the local school. Howie, a devout Christian who is determined to maintain his virginity until marriage, finds himself in conflict with Lord Summerisle (Christopher Lee) who worships pagan gods and believes that the island's crops have failed for lack of a blood sacrifice.

Howie's sensibilities are challenged during his first night on the island. Gaining lodgings at an inn called The Green Man[7], he is met with a curmudgeonly landlord, oafish regulars and a monotonous

Before the darkness: Mickey Rourke and Lisa Bonet in *Angel Heart*'s controversial sex scene.

folk band. All the pub has to commend it is the delectable Willow (Britt Ekland), the landlord's daughter. When Howie turns in, kneeling by his bed to pray, it is Willow's voice he hears murmuring seductively outside his door. She tries the handle. Locked. Howie looks perturbed, but continues his ministrations. The band downstairs strike up a slow, sultry tune. Willow, lying naked on her bed in the next room to Howie's, begins singing to it, tapping her hand in time against the wall.

The song is infused with tactile eroticism ('a stroke as gentle as a feather'). Willow rises from her bed, performing a seductive routine that is half dance, half ritual. As the tempo of the music increases, her movements become wild, feverish. She flings herself upon the connecting door between the two rooms, beating her fists against it. The frankness of her nudity is contrasted with Howie, clad in pyjamas, in the agonies of self-denial.

The dark irony of this scene is evident at the film's chilling conclusion. Howie, singled out from the start, is informed by Lord Summerisle, 'Animals are fine [as a sacrifice], but their acceptability is limited. A small child is even better, but not nearly as effective as the right kind of adult.' In other words, a virgin. Thus, in withstanding the temptation personified by Willow, Howie has sealed his own fate.

Whereas *The Wicker Man* juxtaposes differing religious attitudes to sex (Christian/repressed and pagan/ritualistic), **Angel Heart** (Alan Parker, 1987) very much paves the way for *Ginger Snaps* in its portrayal of sex as a loss of control. It begins very much as a shadowy,

New Orleans-set film noir (the period is the mid-Fifties), before veering in its latter stages into the even darker territory of the Mephistophelean horror film. Shambolic but personable private eye Harry Angel (Mickey Rourke) is hired by the enigmatic Louis Cyphre (Robert de Niro) to undertake what seems to be a routine missing person case. Things quickly turn nasty. Every lead Harry unearths is curtailed by a vicious murder. His investigations take him deeper into not only a criminal netherworld, but one which revolves around the supernatural.

Discovering that his quarry, lounge singer Johnny Favorite, has fathered an illegitimate daughter by a Creole woman, he is shocked to witness the girl, Epiphany Proudfoot (Lisa Bonet), participating in a voodoo ritual. Dressed in only a white cotton shift, unbuttoned to her breasts, she holds a chicken aloft and slits its throat with a straight razor. Blood dribbles across her face and throat and breasts. She throws herself to the ground and writhes orgasmically.

Later, when she visits Harry at his hotel room during a heavy rainstorm, the explicit scene that follows is prelude to a series of revelations which bring the film to its darkest twist: the true nature of Harry's identity.

Harry and Epiphany talk briefly, during which it is revealed that Epiphany is 17 years old (an admission that makes the rest of the scene feel even more uncomfortable), then she puts the radio on and asks Harry to dance. Soon she is kissing him. They fall onto the bed and she straddles him. Like Ginger, she has control of the situation at the outset. However, subsequent shots of their lovemaking show them varying positions, alternately assuming and yielding their dominance. The volume of the song on the radio – 'Soul on Fire' by Laverne Baker, a very sultry number – increases as they become more fervent. The storm outside becomes more violent. There are cuts to the various pieces of crockery Harry has placed around the room to compensate for the leaking roof. Water drips from the roof, courses down the walls; droplets burst upon Harry's gun, which he has left on the dressing table, and fill his half-finished glass of Scotch left next to it. The deluge of water matches the intensity of their sex.

As the scene delivers its most erotic moments, Harry and Epiphany in complete abandonment to each other, the film makes its transition from crime thriller to horror as surely as *From Dusk Till Dawn* does with Santanico Pandemonium's seductive dance (see chapter one).

135

The rain turns to blood. The song becomes muted, replaced on the soundtrack by a darker sonority: solemn bass notes giving way to a harsh drumming, a similar music to that used in the voodoo scene. Likewise, the imagery of the blood sacrifice is revisited. Harry experiences a series of seemingly disconnected hallucinations (buried memories, as it transpires), during which his hands fasten around Epiphany's throat and the moment of orgasm becomes a moment of violence. After this, *Angel Heart*'s transition to the horror genre is absolute.

As *Ginger Snaps*, *The Wicker Man* and *Angel Heart* prove, the horror film has provided filmmakers with a canvas on which to explore some of the darkest manifestations of sexuality cinema has to offer.

But there are aspects of sexual representation that are darker and more controversial still; these are considered in the final chapter.

forbidden flesh

CHAPTER FIVE

As we have seen, the horror genre often trades on a fear of sex, either using death as a punishment for licentiousness (the 'have sex and die' ethos of stalk-and-slash films), or exploiting a more Freudian element: fear of the act itself (most strongly evidenced in *The Wicker Man*). Nonetheless, sexual activity in horror movies is usually quite orthodox; one almost pities the teens who, by the intervention of the Freddies and Jasons of this world, are given no chance to progress beyond a few feverish seconds in the missionary position.

But what of films where, instead of sex as a prelude to something unpleasant, it is the very nature of the sexual behaviour in question, or the manner in which it is exhibited, that takes on a dark, immoral or socially unacceptable aspect? This chapter considers such transgressions, beginning with two films adapted from the same material: a key work by one of the most notorious and sexually explicit writers of all time.

Perversion: de Sade and the cinema

The title of Pier Paolo Pasolini's final film[1] ***Salò, or The 120 Days of Sodom*** (1975) gives two points of reference. Salò is a lakeside town in Northern Italy which, towards the end of World War II, became the last outpost of Mussolini's fascist dictatorship. It is also where the director's brother died at the hands of partisans.

The 120 Days of Sodom refers to the novel by the Marquis de Sade. Although unfinished (de Sade abandoned it in favour of a more philosophical narrative, *Aline and Valcour*), the basic premise is thus: four noblemen, tiring of life, decide to repair to a secluded chateau and kill themselves by means of a protracted abandonment to purely carnal pleasures. Naturally, these pleasures are for the most part claimed at the cost of the suffering of others.

Pasolini's film takes the same starting point, only he updates the setting to 1944 and makes his four degenerates, known only by their titles – the President (Umberto Quintavalle), the Duke (Paolo Bonacelli), the Bishop (Giorgio Cataldi) and the Magistrate (Aldo Valletti) – prominent fascists whose politics are as repulsive as their sexual predilections. They are introduced in a scene in which they announce their intention of marrying each other's daughters (thereby 'sealing our destinies forever').

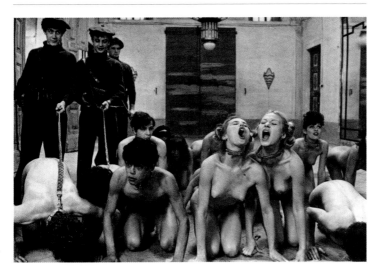

Sexual humiliation in Pasolini's *Salò, or The 120 Days of Sodom*.

Worse is to come.

A group of peasant youths are rounded up, as well as a number of girls (taken from a convent); they are conveyed to an opulent mansion where the four men subject them to all manner of sexual humiliations. On arrival, they are informed that heterosexual acts are punishable by dismemberment, religious acts by death. Whippings and sodomy ensue. They are stripped and enleashed, collars attached to their necks; they are made to act like dogs and eat scraps from bowls.

Still worse awaits.

Enforced acts of coprophilia and urolagnia[2] occur. The victims, utterly depersonalized, either exhibit a disturbing complaisance, or turn against each other, informing on minor infringements to curry favour with their captors. Thus Pasolini orchestrates his material as a shattering statement not only against fascism but also in condemnation of those who collaborate.

He also criticizes bourgeois degeneracy, much in the manner of Buñuel but using imagery even more grotesque than that of the Surrealist. The suggestion of incestuous union in the opening scenes – the first transgression of social acceptability by the noblemen – is compounded by no less than three scenes which make a mockery of marriage. Two are homosexual in nature, with overtones of transvestitism (the 'bride' decked out in traditional dress). The other has two of the captives, boy and girl, forced to enact a wedding ceremony after having been robbed of their virginity in homosexual acts. Afterwards, they are denied consummation – 'no, that flower belongs to us!' – and raped anally.

It is through this defilement of the sanctity of marriage, this utter rejection of love and tenderness, that Pasolini condemns, equally, bourgeois complacency and fascist inhumanity. These political and social denouncements give *Salò* its aesthetic, notwithstanding that Pasolini's often unwatchable catalogue of depravities remain true to de Sade's nihilistic vision.

Marco Ferreri, in **La Grande Bouffe** (1973), also contemporizes the setting (present-day France). His overprivileged quartet are not noblemen, but a renowned chef (Ugo Tognazzi), a TV anchorman (Michel Piccoli), an airline pilot (Marcello Mastroianni) and a judge (Philippe Noiret); all the characters have the same forenames as the actors playing them. Ferreri's most radical departure from the novel is that they decide to kill themselves not by sexual means (Marcello's acquisition of a trio of hookers is merely an afterthought), but by culinary overindulgence. What follows is akin to the banquet scene in *Tom Jones* (see chapter one) stretched to a two-hour running time.

Like Buñuel and Blier (see chapter three), Ferreri organizes the material as an attack on the middle classes and the establishment (hence the respective professions of his protagonists). The greed of the nouveau riche is visualized in the most literal of terms: four people, already overfed, gorging on a vast array of high-calorie fare. 'It's disgusting,' one of the hookers declares, 'eating when you're not hungry.'

Soon their 'guests' depart, utterly sickened. Only one woman remains, a statuesque schoolteacher (Andréa Ferréol) who proves herself their equal in both dining room- and bedroom-based debauchery. (Another satirical touch: the hookers demonstrate integrity while a teacher happily abandons her duties in favour of profligacy.) Moreover, having slept with and out-eaten all of them, she is the only one still alive as the film ends, the men having achieved their aim.

For all the nudity provided in the early scenes by the hookers (one of them, anorexic and barely able to watch them dine let alone partake, is made to disrobe and pelted with handfuls of cake), it is Andréa who draws together the main themes of food, sex and death. With Marcello and Michel already dead, she and Philippe officiate at Ugo's deathbed (not technically a bed, but the kitchen worktop).

While Philippe feeds him large forkfuls of paté, Andréa masturbates him. He dies engorged: in both senses of the word.

As absurd as it is grotesque, *La Grande Bouffe* often seems like a comedic, politically unmotivated, version of *Salò*. And yet it emerges, if anything, as a truer testament to de Sade's concept: unlike Pasolini's film, where the Duke et al are still resolutely alive at the end, Ferreri's characters succeed in their complete and irreversible rejection of life itself.

Incest

Set against a backdrop of burnt-out Eighties yuppiedom and the ill-fated London Docklands development, **Close My Eyes** (Stephen Poliakoff, 1991) uses this atmosphere of economic and social decay as an effective metaphor for the moral debilitation of its characters. Separated at a young age after their parents divorce, Richard (Clive Owen) is reunited with his sister Natalie (Saskia Reeves) in adulthood and their attraction is instant. Natalie is married to an older man, Sinclair (Alan Rickman), a union that seems to be one of convenience. Sinclair, a scion of the upper-middle classes, is everything that Richard aspires to. Having gone through his idealistic, student phase ('I tried to save the planet,' he says at a job interview, vis-à-vis his time unaccounted for), he is desperately trying to scale the corporate ladder. His attraction to Natalie throws the perspective he has just gained on his life into complete disarray. That she feels the same way further clouds the moral no-man's-land in which he finds himself.

Visiting him at his apartment, Natalie soon finds herself in a passionate clinch with Richard. The passion and physicality on display rival any orthodox romantic drama. In fact, in a film where the characters weren't related, it could almost pass for the kind of scene a director would reserve for the finale, all barriers surpassed, all differences resolved, an intimate expression of mutual affection sealing the deal. Here, though, the implications are darker. For a start, both Richard and Natalie are aware from the outset that what they are doing is not just socially unacceptable but illegal (later, stumbling towards a nervous breakdown, Richard obsesses about the potential penal repercussions). 'We mustn't,' Natalie says at several points. But they do. The desire, the need, is too strong. The characters' discomfort is transferred just as potently to the audience. In filming the scene thus – with the emphasis on the absolute power of physical attraction – Poliakoff creates an incredibly tense and emotionally complex scene. Added to this, his actors are both striking in their looks: Owen's brooding intensity has seldom been better used; Reeves exudes a combination of sensuality and deeply felt emotionalism. Thus the audience's responses become as important as Richard and Natalie's behaviour. The issue of complicity is introduced.

But even guilt by association on the part of the audience is nothing compared to the guilt Natalie comes to experience. Disturbed by what she has been a part of, scared by the burgeoning obsession her brother is demonstrating, she refuses to continue their liaisons, insisting that Richard find a girlfriend and move on. His reactions are self-destructive. He loses his grip on the life he has begun to build for himself. In having sexual relations with his sister, he crosses a line, both morally and legally; in cuckolding Sinclair, he spurns the affluent, class-based lifestyle he was aiming for. Poliakoff delivers a telling image towards the end of the film: Richard blundering drunkenly across the wasteland his company is supposed to be redeveloping, a JCB almost crushing him as it demolishes the few remnants that are still standing.

Preceded by *Through a Glass Darkly* (1961) and *Winter Light* (1962), **The Silence** (1963) completes a sequence which is critically considered to constitute Ingmar Bergman's trilogy on faith. The silence is that of God, and every frame of the film is a metaphor for a godless world. It begins with Ester (Ingrid Thulin) and Anna (Gunnel Lindblom), two sisters united and finally divided by an act of incest that has thrown its shadow over their entire adult lives, taking a journey by train, accompanied by Anna's young son Johan (Jorgen Lindstrom), to an unidentified, vaguely eastern European city which is either under occupation or threatened by war. Armaments trains thunder past the passenger express as they approach the station and tanks rumble through the square that the hotel they fetch up at overlooks. Bergman never explains the political situation: it is just another metaphor. The train, with its stern guards, signs in a foreign language and lack of air-conditioning (the nameless city is sweltering under a heatwave), is the long dark night of the characters' souls. It takes them to a state of guilt, confrontation and (for Ester, who is entering the terminal stages of an equally unidentified disease) death.

The hotel, empty but for a troupe of midget circus performers and a concierge whose attentions to Johan might be more than avuncular, is purgatory with room service.

Although Bergman never openly depicts their incest, the fact that such acts have occurred between them permeates the whole film. The fact that Anna also has a son (i.e. she has had other relationships in her life) indicates why their relationship is approaching endgame. Ester,

Emotional emptiness: a shatteringly cynical view of human relationships in Bergman's *The Silence*.

cerebral and buttoned-down, tries to impose a repressive and intellectual degree of control over her sister's life, while Anna, blowsy and overtly sexual, tries to distance herself from their shared guilt by abandonment in heterosexual encounters. In becoming such polar opposites, both have sacrificed their emotionalism.

The turning point is when Anna leaves Ester (by now bed-ridden) and Johan (who occupies himself wandering the deserted corridors of the rambling hotel), and goes into the city. She attends a cabaret theatre where the dwarves are performing. Herself apart, it is empty but for a couple in the back row who have just touched first base. Distracted from the stage show, she watches as the couple get more intimate (they end up openly having sex in their seat). Anna then picks up a stranger at a bar and they meet back at the hotel. The impersonal nature of their encounter – the very definition of casual sex – is made apparent when Anna says to him afterwards, in respect of the language barrier, 'How nice that we don't understand each other.'

It is at this point, as the man commences foreplay with her again, that Ester discovers them *in flagrante*. The long-delayed confrontation occurs, Anna finally repelling her sister. Ester withdraws. Anna goes through a range of emotions, from manic laughter at her (apparent) victory over Ester (Ester will shortly be dead, anyway) to tears of bitter regret, while her lover, oblivious, continues to use her sexually.

Through this scene, Bergman makes his darkest pronouncement on the human condition. This is a world in which incest has replaced

143

sisterly love; in which the lonely figure of a young boy abandoned in a strange building denotes an absence of maternal love; in which emotional intimacy is replaced by voyeurism and casual, quickly forgotten acts of gratification.

While the theme of David O Russell's **Spanking the Monkey** (1994) is incest, the title is a euphemism for masturbation. And indeed, self-abuse provides a running joke through the film as college student Ray (Jeremy Davies), confined to his parents' house during a long hot summer in order to care for his mother, tries to find an outlet for his rampant hormones. His bathroom-based onanism sessions are invariably interrupted by the family dog. His relationship with girlfriend Toni (Carla Galio) is going nowhere: there is no emotional connection and his clumsy attempts at seduction are roundly refuted.

His mother, Susan (Alberta Watson), a 40-something who is still very attractive, is laid up with a broken leg. His father, Tom (Benjamin Hendrickson), is a career-obsessed bully. It is he who blithely leaves town on business, indifferent to his wife's needs, while sanctimoniously lecturing Ray, who is forced to turn down an internship, that becoming nurse to his mother is his duty: 'Sometimes … you have to give a little back.'

Ray's relationship with Susan is initially fractious. To mask his discomfort at not only having to carry her into the shower but be on call to pick up the soap whenever she drops it, he makes a facetious comment about her birthmark. In retaliation, she recounts a story of boyhood bathtime erection ('the boner boat') that leaves him crimson with embarrassment. Gradually, though, they become closer to each other, chiefly – in an inevitable mutual admission – because they have grown to detest Tom for his domineering, self-obsessed personality.

Finally, as they get progressively drunk together one evening, conversation turns to how things are going between Ray and his girlfriend Carla. He complains that she is unresponsive. Susan asks what approaches Ray has made. He demonstrates. Susan berates him for his functional approach to kissing and the complete absence of anything tactile or tender in his technique.

> **Susan:** You've got to be gentle. You know how to be gentle? [She caresses his arm.] Feel this? That's how you touch her. Feel her skin. Smell her hair.

Later, unable to sleep, Ray wanders into his mother's room. She, too, is still awake, complaining of a pain in her hip. Unasked, Ray begins to massage her upper thigh, using lotion, working his fingers under the fabric of her shorts. Adjusting her robe, Susan looks back over her shoulder. Something passes between them. Ray slides on top of her.

Russell does not linger on the scene, but the implications reverberate through the rest of the film. Like Richard in *Close My Eyes*, Ray spirals into a maelstrom of guilt and depression. Eventually, like Tomek in *A Short Film About Love*, he attempts suicide.

Necrophilia

If a film can be said to test the boundaries of acceptability, then Alfred Hitchcock's **Vertigo** (1958) was a risk-taker of the highest order. Released over a year before Michael Powell's *Peeping Tom* (1960) – subject matter: serial murder, scoptophilia, pornography, psychological abuse of a child – incited so much controversy it destroyed its director's career, *Vertigo* if anything edges into even murkier territory. But, as he would go on to do with *Psycho* (1960), Hitchcock delivered his darkest moments with such panache and subtlety that his vision not only avoided a *Peeping Tom*-like backlash, but garnered critical acclaim[3].

A publicity still for *Vertigo* plays on the duality of its heroine.

For a film so drenched in sexuality, there is not a single explicit moment on screen. The psychological darkness of the last half hour is established by a fairly routine private-eye narrative. After a rooftop chase that sees a fellow police officer killed, John 'Scottie' Ferguson (James Stewart) is afflicted with a fear of heights. He retires from the force. An old friend, industrialist Gavin Elster (Tom Helmore), employs him to shadow his wife, Madeleine (Kim Novak), who he believes is acting strangely. Blonde, stylish and possessed of an hourglass figure, Madeleine enchants Ferguson, who drifts into a protective relationship with her. When she dies, ostensibly by taking her own life, Ferguson (who, incapable of climbing the bell tower she fell from, was therefore unable to save her) goes to pieces.

Three years on, he encounters Judy Barton (Novak) – a woman who, except that she's brunette, is Madeleine's look-alike. The revelation that Judy and Madeleine are one and the same is something Hitchcock shares only with the audience. Ferguson does not realize the truth until much later, by which time he has driven Judy towards her destruction through the sheer force of his obsession. The revelation of Judy's identity clarifies her motivations – guilt over her part in Elster's deception, a ploy by which he stages his wife's murder as suicide – and explains why she allows herself to be put through Ferguson's indignities.

With a disturbing lack of emotionalism, he remakes her in Madeleine's image, dressing her in the same outfits and insisting she dye her hair blonde. (His actions are no different to what Don Jaime does in *Viridiana* (see chapter three), remaking a living woman in the image of a dead one in order to make love to her.) The moment when Judy appears as Madeleine is amongst the most chilling that cinema has to offer. The setting is her cheap hotel room, permanently bathed in green from the neon light outside. It is from this surreal glow that Judy emerges – and there is no doubt that the woman Ferguson takes into his arms is Madeleine. Wordlessly, their embrace turns into a kiss, the camera circling them. The hotel room is replaced by a darkness, which embraces them both (highly symbolic, since this is the point at which Ferguson crosses the line). Darkness gives way to a dim half-light and the scene shifts seamlessly to the coach-house at the hacienda where Madeleine committed suicide.

Notwithstanding that it has already been revealed that more than half of the film is sleight of hand – an elaborate con trick – Ferguson is unaware. He believes that Madeleine is dead; that Judy is a different woman, albeit a virtual doppelgänger. It is this context that makes the concluding scenes of *Vertigo* devastating. Not only is Hitchcock's most flawed, most psychologically disturbed hero essayed by James Stewart, star of such moralistic, all-American, feel-good fare as Frank Capra's *Mr Smith Goes to Washington* (1939) and *It's a Wonderful Life* (1946), but his obsession leads him to an act that can be considered – not literally, but certainly psychologically – as necrophilia.

Quills (Philip Kaufman, 2000) gives a more direct portrayal of the act. For a mainstream film with established stars, produced by a major studio (Twentieth Century Fox), the subject matter is dark and subversive. Not only is the main character the Marquis de Sade (Geoffrey Rush), but he is presented as the hero by default, a victim of censorship and suppression. Incarcerated in a lunatic asylum after his explicit writings have caused outrage, he persuades chambermaid Madeleine (Kate Winslet) to smuggle in paper and ink so that he can continue his work.

The asylum is run by Coulmier (Joaquin Phoenix), a priest of liberal and humanitarian views, who attempts to reason with de Sade and persuade him to admit the error of his ways. Without success. Relieved of his duties, kept on in a purely ecumenical role, Coulmier is replaced by Royer-Collard (Michael Caine), a doctor whose cruelty and rampant egomania are on a par with anything in de Sade's fiction. His methods for curing the Marquis amount to little more than state-sanctioned torture. Nonetheless, de Sade engages him in a battle of attrition.

Coulmier, meanwhile, struggles with his conscience, horrified by Royer-Collard's behaviour, particularly towards Madeleine, whom he orders whipped on discovering that she has provided de Sade with writing materials. Coulmier intercedes, offering himself in her place. He grows close to her, and becomes further troubled by the attraction he feels.

During de Sade's final revolt against Royer-Collard, a riot erupts and the inmates overrun the asylum. The innocent victim in all of this is Madeleine. She is attacked by one of them and killed. Once order is restored, Royer-Collard embarks upon a series of abuses against de Sade, through which he finally dies. Coulmier, too, is destroyed, torn apart by grief over Madeleine. Her body is laid out in the chapel, covered by a winding sheet. Coulmier goes there to pay his last respects. He draws the sheet away to uncover her face; then further, revealing that she is naked. He takes her head in his hands. Her eyes open and she wordlessly beckons him. They kiss. She caresses him. He clambers on top of her, assuming (appropriately enough) the missionary position. She wraps her legs around his back.

A voice calls out his name, and Coulmier glances up, horrified. When he looks back down, it is not a living, beautiful woman in his arms, but a hideously mutilated corpse. He looks up again; an effigy of Christ gazes down on him, its lifeless eyes mirroring his guilt.

Quills goes beyond *Vertigo* in depicting the obsessive love of a man for a woman who is dead, but still contrives to let the audience off (i.e. not make them complicit in what they have witnessed) by presenting the act as a fantasy sequence. That Madeleine is 'seen' (however subjectively) to be alive and responding consensually allows the film-makers to present abhorrence in a palatable manner.

Few films have ever crossed the line and shown, absolutely and clinically, an instance of necrophilia[4]. **Kissed** (Lynne Stopkewich, 1996) arguably stands alone as a measured, thoughtful and non-exploitative statement on the subject. As a character study of its protagonist, Sandra (Molly Parker), it begins by probing her childhood: death-fixated from an early age, she stages elaborate funerals for dead animals, carefully interring them. As a young woman, she studies pathology while working at a funeral parlour. Fellow student Matt (Peter Outerbridge) attempts to instigate a relationship with her; despite her inability to function socially (i.e. with people who are still alive), she is able eventually to communicate openly with him, taking him into her confidence as regards her developing sexual interest in the dead. Naturally Matt is shocked, but nonetheless they drift towards a normal relationship.

Things end badly, though, when Sandra's interest in one of the corpses leads to actual intercourse. Her affair with Matt suffers and – in an act of romantic obsession that is as rash and hot-headed as Sandra's expression of sexuality is cold and removed – he takes the drastic step of hanging himself in order to be with her. As grim as this denouement is, it is overshadowed by *Kissed*'s most controversial and challenging scene, which occurs mid-way through the film.

Alone in the embalming room, Sandra examines the next body she is due to prepare: a young man, victim of an accident, his looks and physique still at this point as striking as they were in life. Sandra circles the embalming table. She begins to remove her clothes. Beneath the fluorescent lighting, her skin appears as pallid as that of the corpse. Naked, she continues moving round and round, almost as if bringing herself to a state of trance. Finally, she eases herself onto the table and straddles the body. Stopkewich does not linger on the scene. Moreover, she uses the sterile metallic surfaces of the embalming room to throw back the hard fluorescent light, creating a surreal visual barrier between the audience and what is occurring on screen, glazing a cold whiteness across this darkest of acts.

Sex and religion

There can be little argument that necrophilia is probably the greatest social taboo: a perversion, and a crime against the eternal rest of one who has died. Whatever one's religious beliefs, there is in death a sense of sanctity.

It is paradoxical, then, that even the explicit depiction of the act in *Kissed* generated less controversy than, say, Ken Russell's **The Devils** (1971), whose imagery was considered so blasphemous that an entire sequence was excised and remained lost for over 30 years. Based on historical events which had already been recounted in Aldous Huxley's book *The Devils of Loudon* and dramatized in John Whiting's play *The Devils* (both are acknowledged in the credits), Russell's film portrays the attempts of Father Grandier (Oliver Reed) to defend Loudon from the political chicanery of Cardinal Richelieu (Christopher Logue), who seeks to tear down the city walls and leave it defenceless. Grandier, though a good man in many respects, is vain and has a weakness for women. This is his downfall. Richelieu's emissaries, Baron de Laubardemont (Dudley Sutton) and Father Barre (Michael Gothard), use these traits to discredit him. Their case is bolstered by the allegations of Sister Jeanne (Vanessa Redgrave), the hunchbacked leader of a convent of Ursuline nuns. Jeanne lusts after Grandier, but because of her physical defect knows that her desires will never be requited. When he turns down her offer of the position of Father Confessor at the convent (the prissy Father Mignon (Murray Melvin) is appointed in his stead) she accuses Grandier of having congress with Satan, and sexual relations with the nuns under her charge.

Jeanne's sexual hysteria is reflected in the behaviour of the other nuns, most of who are unmarriageable young women, sent to the convent because a dowry cannot be raised for them. Barre exploits them, staging a mock exorcism (he has already instructed them, on

Publicity stills for *The Devils* expose the juxtaposition of religious imagery and sexual hysteria.

pain of execution, to behave as if possessed). By this means, Barre creates outrage, turning the tide of public opinion against Grandier, whom he then has arrested, tried (before the ecclesiastical equivalent of a kangaroo court), and burned at the stake.

As harrowing as Grandier's death is, it is during the 'exorcism' that Russell conjures his most extreme imagery. What finally made it into cinemas is graphic enough – full-frontal nudity, masturbation, pages torn from the Bible and burned – but his original cut contained a sequence so contentious that it was removed in its entirety. A sequence that became so fabled in film lore that it earned itself its own title: 'the rape of Christ'.

Astoundingly, it resurfaced in late 2002, unearthed by the film critic Mark Kermode. Screened in its entirety as part of the Channel 4 documentary *Hell on Earth: The Desecration and Resurrection of 'The Devils'*, the two-and-a-half minute sequence shows an effigy of Christ, three times the size of a man, taken down from a wall. A group of hysterical nuns, all naked, straddle it and simulate sexual acts on the face, torso, and genital area of the statue. As the frenzy reaches its climax, Mignon, watching from an upper storey of the cathedral, vigorously masturbates under his cassock.

Mignon's self-abuse can be seen as a metaphor for the abuses of church and state, as well as a direct riposte by the director to anyone in the audience who might consider his *mise en scènes* arousing. As extreme as the 'rape of Christ' sequence is, the film is thematically weakened as a result of its removal. Without it, the serious and valid points Russell is making about the corruption and perversion of office are made more palatable, and thus less effective.

Losing a sequence is one thing. An offer by a fundamentalist Christian to recompensate the entire budget of a film in return for the destruction of the negative is quite something else. This was just one of many headline-grabbing incidents surrounding Martin Scorsese's ***The Last Temptation of Christ*** (1988). Adapted from the novel by Nikos Kazantzakis, it is a profound and intelligent work by a director who considered entering the seminary before he became a filmmaker. A pre-credits title-card advises that it is a work of fiction and not an adaptation of the gospels. The ending – which sees Jesus reconciled with God having withstood temptation and sacrified Himself for mankind – is arguably one of the most moving scenes in cinema.

Sadly, there were those who did not see it that way (some of whom, in point of fact, began protesting about the film before they had even seen it). Scorsese first attempted to develop the project at Paramount studios in 1983. His efforts came to nothing. Other studios passed. Finally, bankrolled by Universal, principal photography commenced in Morocco in 1987. Even while the film was still being shot, media controversy got underway. In June 1988, a fundamentalist Christian named Tim Penland (hired by Universal as an advisor) made a very public resignation from the production, protesting the non-availability of a rough cut of the film, which he had been promised he could screen for his fellow fundamentalists. The simple fact was that the production was slightly behind schedule and a rough cut was, at that point, unavailable. Nonetheless, the press lapped it up.

The following month, Christian societies lodged complaints with Lew Wasserman, CEO of Universal's parent company MCA; Universal studios were picketed; and Bill Bright, a wealthy fundamentalist, made the aforementioned fiscal offer for the film's destruction. All this before its release!

The incidents that greeted its release upped the ante. Protestations and calls to boycott the film were rife in the US. Cinemas screening it were subject to vandalism. In the UK, Mary Whitehouse (predictably) urged for bans to be implemented by local councils. London Transport announced a ban on the film's poster. Rioting occurred in Paris; distribution was eventually withdrawn in France. The film was banned outright in Greece and Israel.

These occurrences were all incited by one self-contained section of the film. The temptation sequence – so crucial to the aesthetic that it gives both novel and film their title – begins with the crucifixion of Jesus (Willem Dafoe). Suffering, mocked by the crowds who have gathered to watch Him die, He cries out to God: 'Why have you forsaken me?' As if in answer, an angel appears to Him in the form of a young girl (Juliette Caton). She removes the nails, kisses His wounds and brings Him down from the cross. Telling Him He is not the Messiah, she leads Him to a bucolic and peaceful valley where wedding preparations are in progress. 'Whose?' He enquires. 'Yours,' comes the reply.

And this is the nature of His temptation: to live as a normal man. We see Him take as His wife Mary Magdalene (Barbara Hershey); on their wedding night He lies naked in her arms as she bathes His wounds. This done, they make love. There is nothing carnal or exploitative about Scorsese's handling of the scene; it is tastefully shot and not lingered on. Physical love is shown as an act of human tenderness, a good and natural thing. For this, after all, is part of His temptation: to enjoy the experience of humanity, instead of suffering for the redemption thereof. His decision, in the closing moments, to return to the Cross, to suffer and die upon it so that a greater good can prevail, is thus the reaffirmation of the spiritual – a true statement of profound religious belief – that the film's critics seem to overlook.

Scorsese, in a statement issued at the height of the controversy, said, 'My film was made with deep religious feeling ... it is more than just another film project for me. I believe it is a religious film about suffering and the struggle to find God. It was made with conviction and love and so I believe it is an affirmation of faith, not a denial' [5]

afterword

Fançois Truffaut once described cinema as 'truth at twenty-four frames per second'. A laudable sentiment, but is it an accurate one? By its own essence, cinema is an illusion: what is seen on screen is scripted, acted and edited. Cinema is an art form and art is a form of representation.

As we have seen, sex in cinema generally has a narrative purpose. In film noir and horror, it is often a prelude to death. Character-based dramas (*Under the Skin*, for example, or *Breaking the Waves*) portray sex as a form of catharsis. In the hands of (mainly) European directors, sex becomes a subject unto itself: virtually all of the films examined in chapter three are driven or defined by the characters' exploration or expression of their sexual identities.

And of course there are Just Jaeckin, Zalman King and their imitators, in whose works sexual imagery is presented for its own sake. Nonetheless, their films still strive to pay lip service to traditional narrative conventions, using tales of adultery, obsession or voyeurism to string together their lascivious set pieces.

It remains ironic that sex – generally a pleasurable act – is so often depicted negatively in cinema: a thing that has to be paid for, either financially (in films about prostitution/hustling), or in terms of mortality (the aforementioned have-sex-and-die ethos of the horror movie). This discrepancy returns us to Truffaut's definition and a couple of thorny questions.

If cinema is truth – i.e. a document of what is real, actual and absolute (consider the incorporation of hardcore imagery into *The Piano Teacher*) – does this licence filmmakers to show anything?

And if filmmakers achieve free rein in the extremes of what can be shown (advances in special effects and computer-generated imagery have rendered possible the visualization of almost anything), what is left for cinema as an art form? Where does it go next?

NOTES

CHAPTER ONE: IMPLICIT

1 *Double Indemnity*'s screenplay was co-written by its director and Raymond Chandler, one of Cain's contemporaries in the world of hard-boiled fiction.
2 Hayworth was a professional dancer before her move into acting.
3 Maitland McDonagh, *The 50 Most Erotic Films of All Time*, p. 123.
4 It was James Fox's first film role. Six years later, he starred in *Performance* (see chapter two), to which he brings a similar sense of sexual ambiguity.

5 It is worth noting – given that director Richardson (*Look Back in Anger, A Taste of Honey, The Loneliness of the Long-Distance Runner*), scriptwriter John Osborne (*Look Back in Anger*), and star Finney (*Saturday Night and Sunday Morning*) were all associated with the anti-establishment/'angry young man' school of cinema prevalent at the time – that the film, for all its costume-drama trappings, continually attacks class and society as repressive against the individual.

6 It is memorably spoofed in *The Naked Gun 2½* (David Zucker, 1991).

7 A generally derogatory colloquialism meaning a film designed to attract a large female audience.

8 See, for example, sections on *Mulholland Drive* in chapter two and *The Piano* in chapter four.

CHAPTER TWO: EXPLICIT

1 An ironic profession for a resident of a destroyed city.

2 See the author's previous book *One Hundred Violent Films that Changed Cinema* for an analysis of how social disaffection and political protest during the Seventies were reflected in the work of a new wave of film-makers.

3 *Sight and Sound*, volume 11, issue 7 (July 2001).

4 Possibly a homage to Hitchcock's *Vertigo*, where a brunette is remodelled as a blonde (see chapter five).

5 The quixotic Donald Cammell made only four films: *Performance* (co-directed with Nicolas Roeg), *Demon Seed*, *White of the Eye* and *Wild Side*, which was re-edited by the studio following its completion in 1996 and released directly to video, packaged and advertised to exploit its lesbian content. Shortly afterwards, Cammell committed suicide. *Wild Side* was eventually restored to its original cut and re-released in 1999.

6 Ken Russell, *Directing Film*, p. 94.

7 Roeg photographed the film as well as directing.

8 The credits refer to them as Girl, White Boy and Black Boy. In the spirit of our more 'correct' times, I have referred to them as Girl, Boy and Aborigine.

9 Neil Sinyard, *The Films of Nicolas Roeg*, p. 53.

10 It does, however, allow for a witty play on audience preconceptions: when he is accused, part way into the film, of being 'an alien', it takes a moment or two to realize that this is actually a reference to his not having adopted American citizenship.

CHAPTER THREE: THE EUROPEAN AESTHETIC

1 *Venus in Furs* was filmed in 1968 by Massimo Dallamano, and remade a year later by Jess Franco. Neither version amounts to anything more than soft-core pornography. (The novel also influenced the Velvet Underground song of the same name.)

2 The title is a colloquialism for the male scrotum. Given a certain incompatibility of translation, it has been released in England and America as, variously, *Making It* and *Going Places*. In its most recent screening on British television, the indigenous title was restored.

3 One of Marcello's colleagues, a photographer who demonstrates not a shred of dignity or humanity towards his subjects, is called Paparazzo; it is from his name that the derogatory term 'paparazzi' is derived.

4 See the author's previous book *One Hundred Violent Films that Changed Cinema* for an evaluation of the interconnectedness of sex and violence in *Matador*.

CHAPTER FOUR: PLEASURE AND PAYMENT

1 At the time he was cast for *Romance*, Siffredi was already an established star in the hardcore pornography industry.

2 Interestingly, Max's concluding speech, where he declares 'I'm proud of what I did and I'd do it all again' then takes the Nazi salute, was taken from Adolf Eichmann's address to the court during his trial for war crimes in 1961.

3 Narratively, 'Fidelio' is the password by which Harford gains access to the private party. It is also an ironic reference to Beethoven's only opera, which ends with the chorus '*wer ein holdes Weib errungen*', a celebration of marriage. The aesthetic of Kubrick's film, on the other hand, is founded on temptation and unfaithfulness.

4 Evan Hunter, *Me and Hitch*, p. 76.

5 See the section on 'rites of passage' movies in chapter two.

6 With the honourable exceptions of Joe Dante's *The Howling* (1980) and John Landis's *An American Werewolf in London* (1981), it is difficult to bring to mind any werewolf movies that are worthy of note.

7 The name refers to a figure in folklore representative of fertility. The film also uses the image of the Maypole.

CHAPTER FIVE: FORBIDDEN FLESH

1 Before the film's release, Pasolini was murdered by a rent boy.

2 Respectively, sexual gratification gained from acts involving excretion and urination.

3 *Peeping Tom*, by comparison, was not rediscovered and re-evaluated as a masterpiece until the Eighties.

4 Of the very few films which broach the subject, most are horror/exploitation titles such as *Living Doll* (Peter Litten and George Dugdale, 1989), and the German *Nekromantik* series (banned in the UK) directed by Jörg Buttgereit.

5 Quoted in *Scorsese on Scorsese*, introduction, p. xxii.

SELECTED BIBLIOGRAPHY

Bogarde, Dirk. *An orderly man.* Penguin, 1992.

Hunter, Evan. *Me and Hitch.* Faber & Faber, 1997.

McDonagh, Maitland. *The 50 most erotic films of all time.* Citadel Press, 1996.

Russell, Ken. *Directing film.* B T Batsford, 2001.

Sinyard, Neil. *The films of Nicolas Roeg.* Charles Letts & Co, 1991.

Thompson, David and Ian Christie. *Scorsese on Scorsese.* Faber & Faber, 1989.

Sight and Sound, volume 11 issue 7 (July 2001), 'Last Tango in Lewisham' by Richard Falcon.

ACKNOWLEDGEMENTS

My thanks to the following for permission to quote from copyright materials: Faber & Faber for *Scorsese on Scorsese* edited by David Thompson and Ian Christie, and *Me and Hitch* by Evan Hunter; B T Batsford for *Directing Film* by Ken Russell; *Sight and Sound* for an excerpt from the article 'Last Tango in Lewisham' by Richard Falcon.

Thanks to Tina Persaud, Teresa Howes and Niamh Hatton at Batsford for their continued support.

A mention in dispatches to the following: my Mother and Father, Viv and Dennis Apple, Richard Cox, Anthony Dean, Michael Eaton, Robert Kenchington, Mark Miller, Carole Parnell, Judith Rose, Alex Thompson and Rob Varley; the 'usual suspects' at the NWC; and the Broadway Cinema, Nottingham.

INDEX